BEDE

Celtic and Roman
Christianity in Britain

BEDE

Celtic and Roman Christianity in Britain

Edited by

Robert Van de Weyer

ARTHUR JAMES

BERKHAMSTED

First published in 1997 by

ARTHUR JAMES LTD
70 Cross Oak Road
Berkhamsted
Hertforshire HP4 3HZ

A catalogue record for this book is available
from the British Library.

ISBN 0 85305 409 6

Typeset in Monotype Joanna by
Strathmore Publishing Services, London N7

Printed in Great Britain by
The Guernsey Press Company Ltd, Guernsey, C.I.

Contents

Editor's Introduction   1

Bede's Introduction   9

Part 1   Lucius and Alban:
the Arrival of the Gospel   11

Part 2   Gregory and Augustine:
the Gospel in Kent   20

Part 3   Paulinus and Edwin:
the Gospel in York   30

Part 4   Columba, Aidan and Oswald:
the Gospel in Northumbria   37

Part 5   Felix, Fursey and Etheldreda:
the Gospel in East Anglia   44

Part 6   Cedd, Earconwald and Ethelburga:
the Gospel in Essex   49

Part 7   Hilda, Wilfred and Caedmon:
Conflicts and Visions at Whitby   56

Part 8   Theodore and Hadrian:
Laws and Doctrines at Hertford   65

Part 9   Chad and Coenred:
the Gospel in Mercia   72

Part 10   Wilfred: the Abbot of Ripon   80

Part 11   Cuthbert: the Hermit of Farne Island   86

Part 12   John: the Healer of Beverley   102

Bede: Celtic and Roman Christianity in Britain

Part 13	Wilbrord and the Hewalds: the Gospel in Frisia	107
Part 14	Biscop: the Abbot of Wearmouth	111
Part 15	Ceolfrid: the Abbot of Jarrow	121
Epilogue	The Death of Bede: By a Disciple	127
Appendix 1	The Main Figures	130
Appendix 2	The Main Places	139
Bibliography		145
Index	References to the Original Texts	147

Editor's Introduction

Fourteen centuries ago, in 597, Columba died on the island of Iona. He had brought from Ireland a style of Christianity generally called 'Celtic'. He himself went on missions to the Picts and Scots; and later a monk from Iona, Aidan, brought Celtic Christianity down to Northumbria. Also in 597 Augustine landed at Thanet in Kent. He had been sent by Pope Gregory to bring to Britain the style of Christianity practised in Rome. Augustine and his followers, despite various setbacks, gradually extended their influence northwards. The rivalry between Celtic and Roman Christianity reached its first climax at the Synod of Whitby in 664. And it may be argued that religion in Britain since that period has been marked by a continual tension – sometimes creative, sometimes destructive – between the Celtic and the Roman spirit.

Our primary source of knowledge of early Christianity in Britain is the work of Bede, a saintly and scholarly monk of the early eighth century. He was a meticulous historian, recording only those incidents and events for which there was solid evidence. But he was a devout Christian and an imaginative writer, who wished to uplift his readers with stories of saintly exploits. Thus Bede has preserved for us some of the most loveable and inspiring characters of all time. Stories from Bede – such as the martyrdom of Alban, Pope Gregory's encounter with Anglo-Saxon slaves, Cuthbert's relations with the birds on Farne Island, Caedmon's discovery of the gift of song – have been re-told to generation after generation of children, and their souls have been nourished by them.

Yet few return to the source, and many remain unaware of it; the stories seem simply to be part of our cultural heritage, alongside those of King Arthur and Robin Hood. The reason is that Bede's historical writings are surprisingly hard to read. Although he was eager to record the dates when events occurred, he often does not present events in chronological order, making the narrative confused. And the way in which he interweaves different strands of his tale is designed more for theological argument than for ease of understanding. Moreover the characters and incidents which capture our attention are often surrounded by material which to the modern reader seems arcane and irrelevant.

This book is an attempt to bring Bede himself to a wider audience. I have to a degree reordered and abridged his work, in order to make the narrative easier to follow. Very occasionally, where there are important gaps in Bede's narrative, I have filled these gaps with one or two sentences from other contemporary sources. And I have divided it into chapters, focusing on particular people and on the various kingdoms within Britain. When read from cover to cover I believe this presentation of Bede is as compelling as any novel or work of history. Equally Bede's work – at least in the parts I have selected – has something of the flavour of the Gospels: each short event or episode contains lessons and truths on which we can reflect. For this reason I have sub-divided the text into short numbered paragraphs, which can be used as daily readings. These numbers also serve, via an index, as a reference to Bede's original chapters.

No amount of re-ordering of Bede's work can alter the large number of characters that move in and out of his narrative. And just as in a Russian novel, many of the names seem bewilderingly alike, so the modern reader of Bede can find many of the old Anglo-Saxon names hard to distinguish. Thus I have added an appendix giving an alphabetical list of the main figures, and brief biographical notes, to which the reader can refer whenever necessary. There is also an appendix of place names, to help the reader with the geography of Bede's Britain. This 'remote island', as he often calls Britain, was divided into a number of separate kingdoms, which sometimes went to war with one another and sometimes bound themselves together with royal marriages. The kingdoms with which Bede mainly deals were on the eastern half of what we now call England; this was where the Anglo-Saxons were most dominant – and it is the Anglo-Saxons, as distinct from the ancient Britons whom they subjugated, that are Bede's main focus of interest.

In marked contrast to the lives of his heroes, Bede's own life was quietly uneventful. He was born in 672 or 673 near the Northumbrian coast. Shortly after his birth the land where his parents lived was given by the king of Northumbria to a monk called Biscop, on which to found a monastery. And at the age of seven Bede was entrusted by his parents to Biscop's care. From that moment until his death Bede lived under monastic discipline. Initially Bede lived at Biscop's first monastery, on the mouth of the River Wear. But when in 685 Biscop started a second monastery at Jarrow, with Ceolfrid as abbot, Bede was sent there. A year later, when Bede was barely fourteen years old, a plague struck Jarrow, killing all the members of the monastery except Ceolfrid and Bede himself. For a period this man and boy maintained the daily round of monastic worship, praying God to send others to join them.

After this catastrophe the monasteries at both Jarrow and Wearmouth grew rapidly, so that by the time of Ceolfrid's death thirty years later they had a combined total of six hundred monks. Bede was ordained deacon in his nineteenth year, and made priest eleven years later. Thereafter, by his own testimony, he devoted himself to reading, writing and teaching. He was extremely fortunate in that both Biscop and Ceolfrid encouraged scholarship, and to this end accumulated large numbers of books. Thus Bede had access to what was probably the best library in Britain. In Bede's estimation, his most important works were his Biblical commentaries, covering almost the entire Old and New Testaments. And judging by the number of copies of these that were made in the following decades and centuries, these were extremely popular. For example 95 manuscripts of his commentary on St Mark's Gospel are known to exist, and 110 manuscripts on the Pastoral Epistles. His intended readers were priests and monks, who had a virtual monopoly of literacy. But his purpose was not simply their edification; he worked to help them become better pastors and teachers of the common people. So he often used homely metaphors, drawn from daily life, to illustrate his points. In one famous passage, in his commentary on the first book of Samuel, he compares our different ways of spiritual understanding with different methods of cooking: when we are constantly turning theological ideas over in our minds, it is like cooking in a frying-pan; when we meditate slowly, it is like cooking in an oven; and when we seek to apply our faith to practical problems, and thus protect ourselves from the forces of evil, it is like cooking on a griddle – which gives a good and hard surface.

Bede's first major historical work was his *Life of Cuthbert*. The first *Life of Cuthbert* was written by an anonymous monk in 700, only thirteen years after the saint's death; and it was a series of anecdotes based on personal recollections. However, the monks at Lindisfarne, where Cuthbert had been abbot, regarded the life as inadequate in both style and content; and they asked Bede to write a more worthy tribute. He initially composed a long poem about Cuthbert; then, in around 720, he produced a prose biography. The latter included a great deal of new material, provided by the monks who knew Cuthbert. A little later, in around 725, Bede wrote the *Lives of the Abbots of Wearmouth and Jarrow*. The two central figures of this book, Biscop and Ceolfrid, were the major formative influences on Bede himself; and his intense love and respect for them radiates from the pages. But, far from descending into hagiography, Bede offers a balanced account of their achievements, and gives a fascinating glimpse into contemporary monastic life.

Bede's masterpiece, *A History of the English Church and People*, was written at the behest of the abbot of the monastery in Canterbury which Augustine had founded just over a century earlier. The abbot not only sent various historical documents to

Bede, but also arranged for an English priest to go to Rome and transcribe from the papal archives letters written and received by Pope Gregory in connection with the English mission. Bede for his part corresponded with various bishops and abbots, priests and monks, around Britain to glean further information. And within his native Northumbria Bede was able to talk directly with old men who actually remembered many of the crucial events. Thus Bede's History was an extraordinary feat of research, which in the succeeding decades and centuries won admiration amongst scholars throughout Europe.

But it is far more than a history book; it also combines great literary genius with spiritual insight. Bede did not merely try to record the past; he wanted to bring the heroes and saints of old back to life, so that they could inspire future generations, just as they had inspired their contemporaries. Like all great spiritual teachers – indeed, like Jesus himself – Bede understood that stories, rather than theological propositions, excite the religious imaginations of ordinary people. So he related the stories of Alban and Edwin, Aidan and Cuthbert, Hilda and Caedmon, and all the rest, with consummate skill. And he understood too that, to win the heart of the reader, the writer's heart must be with his subjects. So Bede is unashamed in expressing his love and admiration for these great figures; his book is wonderfully warm and affectionate.

These heroes and their stories are presented by Bede as characters in a double drama: the drama of bringing the Christian gospel to a heathen land; and the dramatic conflict between two great Christian traditions, Celtic and Roman. And this drama is made even more compelling because it is played out within Bede himself: his head is Roman, but his heart remains firmly Celt. The focus of the conflict between Celt and Roman was their different methods of calculating the date of Easter, a matter which at this distance of time seems utterly trivial. But beneath this issue lay two more fundamental differences. The first was Church organisation. The Celts saw the local community – be it the monastery or the village church –

as the basic unit of Christian life; bishops, where they existed, were preachers who travelled from one community to another, encouraging the people in their faith. The Romans, by contrast, regarded the Church as a hierarchy, with the Pope at the top; he in turn appoints archbishops and bishops, who send priests to parishes. Bishops in this system were primarily administrators, rather than preachers, managing both the clergy and the buildings and lands which the Church owned. The second difference was spiritual. The Celts saw a close affinity between human beings and other living creatures, and thus rejoiced in the beauty of God's creation; to the Roman mentality this was fanciful and even downright heretical.

The conflict between Celt and Roman reached its climax at the Synod of Whitby in 664; and Bede's description of this confrontation is the pivotal point in his History. The arguments deployed by Wilfred, the leader of the Roman side, are related in detail; and Colman, the Celt's leader, is presented as stubborn and awkward. Thus Bede leaves no doubt in the reader's mind that the Roman side deserves to win the debate. And both here and elsewhere Bede writes of Wilfred with respect. Yet Wilfred is the least likeable of Bede's heroes, constantly trying to assert his authority and picking quarrels with his opponents; the humility and gentleness, which Bede praises in such figures as Cuthbert and Aidan, is wholly absent in Wilfred. Thus the reader's sympathies remain firmly on the Celtic side.

At the start of the encounter between Celtic and Roman forms of Christianity, the division was racial as well as religious. Augustine was a southern European, probably from Rome itself; and his early allies were Anglo-Saxons, who in the previous two centuries had conquered and subdued much of Britain. His opponents, as Bede stresses, were mostly native Britons; some were descendants of families who had adopted Christianity during the Roman occupation, while others had been converted by missionaries from Ireland. However the mission from Iona into Northumbria, led by Aidan, was instigated by an Anglo-Saxon king of Northumbria, Oswald; and its converts included both the Anglo-Saxon nobility and the British peasantry. Thus by the time of the Synod of Whitby the races were thoroughly mixed. In particular, those on the Celtic side included Anglo-Saxons as well as native Britons.

The most famous passage in this entire History is of a pagan priest in York comparing the human life-span on earth with a sparrow flying into a warm banqueting hall, and then a few moments later flying out again into a cold stormy night; the pagan priest is attracted to Christianity because it helps to explain what happens to us when our brief span is over. To Bede, and to his saints and heroes, the Christian gospel is first and foremost a promise of life after death, in the company of Jesus Christ, for those who obey his commands. Thus not surprisingly some of the most moving, and the most charming, passages in Bede's History are the death scenes. A pattern is set by Alban, who goes to his martyr's death radiant with joy at the prospect of heavenly reward. Then there is Aidan who, knowing that he is dying, insists on having a hut and oratory built for himself near a main road, so he can talk to passers-by; he actually dies leaning against one of the oratory buttresses, waiting for passers-by to come. Etheldreda, who founded Ely, had the gift of prophecy; and accurately predicted the date of her death seven years in advance. Hilda, who founded Whitby, was ill for seven years before she died; and through her long, painful illness she changed from being a superb administrator to being a saint. Chad chose to start a monastery in a place where evil spirits were most powerful; and having defeated those spirits through prayer and fasting, he was happy to die there. The dying Cuthbert argued with his brethren about the place of his burial; since people – wrongly in his view – regarded him as a saint, he did not want to be buried at Lindisfarne, for fear that pilgrims to his grave would disturb the peace of the monastery. Biscop, the founder of Wearmouth and Jarrow, preached a stunning sermon just before he died; although he himself had been appointed by the king and the bishop, he insisted that all future abbots should be democratically elected.

Fortunately Bede's own dying hours were recorded. When he realised that death was near, he was in the midst of translating St John's Gospel into the vernacular Northumbrian tongue, so that it could be read out in parish churches. So he accelerated his efforts. During his last night on earth he refused to sleep, and instead continued to dictate his translation to a rota of young monks. The following evening, when death was almost upon him, one of these young monks reminded him that he had not yet translated the final verse of the final chapter. Bede dictated the final verse, chanted the *Gloria*, and breathed his last. So Bede died as he had lived: the humble, devout scholar, striving to make the treasures of the Christian faith accessible to the common people.

To offer a reordered and abridged edition of Bede's historical works may seem like a criticism. In truth it is a tribute. There are very few history books written even one or two centuries ago that can still command our attention; human culture evolves so quickly, that each generation wants the past served to it in a new way. Bede wrote almost thirteen centuries ago, in a culture vastly different from our own; so it is small wonder that some of his material is a little indigestible for the present generation. It is a measure of his extraordinary genius as a historian, a teacher, and also a spiritual sage, that his popularity endures.

Bede's Introduction

I, Bede, the servant of Christ and a priest of the monasteries at
Wearmouth and Jarrow, have written down the following
about the history of the Church in Britain, and of the Church of
the English people in particular. I have assembled the facts from
ancient writings, from traditions handed down by word of
mouth, and from my own personal knowledge. I was born on
land belonging to this monastery; and at the age of seven, I was
entrusted by my parents to the care of Abbot Biscop, and later
Abbot Ceolfrid, for my education. Since then I have remained in
the monastery, devoting myself entirely to the study of the
Scriptures. While I willingly submitted to all the rules of
monastic life, and while I have attended all the services in the
monastery church, my chief delight has always been in study,
writing and teaching. I was ordained deacon in my nineteenth
year, and priest in my thirtieth. From the time of receiving my
priesthood until now I have spent most of my energies, both
for my own benefit and that of my brethren, in compiling short
extracts from the commentaries which the early Fathers wrote
on the Scriptures. I have also written a book of hymns and a
book of epigrams, as well as books on orthography and the art
of poetry. In addition I now offer this historical work.

Part 1

Lucius and Alban: the Arrival of the Gospel

1.1 The Geography of Britain

Britain, formerly known as Albion, is an island in the ocean, lying at a considerable distance north-west of the coasts of Germany, Gaul and Spain, which together form the greater part of Europe. It stretches about 800 miles northwards, and is about 200 miles wide, except in several places where promontories stretch further. Britain is rich in grain and timber, and has good pasture for cattle. Vines are cultivated in various places. It is famous for its plentiful springs and for its rivers abounding in fish; salmon and eels are especially common. It has numerous shell-fish, such as mussels, which contain excellent pearls of all colours, red, purple, violet and green, as well as white. Whelks are also abundant, and a beautiful scarlet dye is extracted from them which never fades. It also has hot springs, which provide water for baths. Beneath the soil there are rich veins of copper, iron, lead and silver. Since Britain lies so far to the north, near the pole, its nights are very short in summer; indeed at midnight it is hard to tell whether the evening twilight still lingers, or the dawn approaches. So the days are long in summer, and the nights are long in winter.

1.2 The Nations and Languages of Britain

At present Britain has four nations and five languages. The four nations are the English, the British, the Scots and the Picts. They each have their own language, but they are united in their study of God's truth by the fifth language, Latin. At first the only inhabitants of the island were the Britons, from whom it takes its name. According to tradition they crossed to the island from Brittany, initially occupying the southern areas, and gradually spreading northwards. Then some Picts set out from Scandinavia in long-boats. Storms carried them to the north coast of Ireland where they found the Scots. They asked if they could settle there. The Scots refused permission, saying that there was not room for both nations. But they added: 'There is another island to the east, which on clear days we can see in the distance. Go and settle there; and if you meet any resistance, we will come to your help.' So the Picts crossed to Britain, and settled in the northern part of the island. Since they had no women with them, the Picts sent a message to Ireland, asking the Scots to provide them with wives. The Scots agreed, on condition that the Picts should always choose their king from the female line, rather than the male. Some time later a large group of Scots, under a chieftain called Reuda, crossed the sea and settled alongside the Picts in northern Britain.

1.3 Caesar's Invasion of Britain

Britain remained unknown and unvisited by the Romans until the time of Julius Caesar, who became consul sixty years before the birth of our Lord. During a campaign against the Germans and the Gauls, he entered the province of Morini, from which is the nearest and quickest crossing to Britain. He assembled eighty ships and sailed to Britain. His forces were routed in a fierce battle; and then a violent storm destroyed much of his fleet, killing many soldiers and horses. He returned to Gaul, and dispersed his legions into winter quarters. He now gave orders for six hundred ships to be built, and in the spring made a second attack on Britain. But after he had landed, and was marching towards the enemy, his fleet was again struck by a violent storm, which destroyed forty ships and damaged many more, dashing them against one another and driving them onto the sands.

At their first charge Caesar's cavalry were defeated by the Britons, and their tribune slain. At their second encounter Caesar's troops were victorious, and continued to march towards the Thames. On the north bank, and under the water at the ford, the Britons had erected sharpened stakes, cased in lead and as thick as a man's thigh. The Romans managed to avoid the stakes, and chased the Britons into the nearby forests. Caesar went on to capture several British strongholds, while the Britons continued to harass the Romans by frequent fierce ambushes. Eventually Caesar was compelled to leave Britain, in order to fight wars in other parts of the Roman empire.

1.4 Lucius, the First British Christian

For a century after Caesar's departure no Roman had dared to land on the island of Britain. Then the emperor Claudius, forty-six years after the birth of our Lord, crossed to Britain with a vast army. Within a few days, without battles or bloodshed, the greater part of the island had surrendered to him. To mark his success, he gave his son the name Britannicus. In the same year the great famine occurred in Syria, recorded in the Acts of the Apostles. Just over a century later, in AD 156, Lucius, a British chieftain, wrote to Eleutherus, the bishop of Rome, asking to be taught the Christian faith. This request was granted; and Lucius and many of his followers were baptised. In this way Christianity came to Britain. Just over three decades later, under the harsh rule of the emperor Severus, many of the tribes of Britain rose up in rebellion. Severus came to Britain and defeated the tribes in southern and middle parts of Britain, but left the northern part unconquered. He then built a wall of earth from the east coast to the west, dividing the Picts and Scots in the north from the rest of Britain.

1.5 Persecution Under Emperor Diocletian

In the year of our Lord 286 Diocletian became emperor. He ruled the eastern half of the empire, and chose Maximian to rule the western half. They appointed Carausius, an able and energetic soldier of humble birth, to protect the eastern coasts of Britain, which were being ravaged by Franks and Saxons. But instead of repelling these pirates, he encouraged their raids, and then took from them a portion of their booty. When he heard what was happening Maximian ordered Carausius to be executed. But Carausius declared himself emperor of Britain, and with great courage held the island for seven years. He was murdered by his colleague Allectus, who ruled Britain for a further three years, eventually succumbing to troops loyal to Maximian.

In the meantime Diocletian and Maximian ordered all churches throughout the empire to be destroyed, and all Christians to be hunted down and killed. This was the tenth persecution which Christians had faced, and lasted longer and was bloodier than all the rest. Over a period of ten years churches were burnt, and countless men, women and children were made martyrs. Eventually the persecution spread to Britain, and the glorious light of martyrdom was to shine even on this remote island.

1.6 *Alban's Arrest*

Alban was a pagan living in Verulanium in southern Britain. When the persecution of Christians began in Britain, a Christian priest came to Alban's house and pleaded for shelter. Alban let him stay; and he was so impressed with the priest's strict routine of prayer and vigil, that he wanted to follow the priest's example. The priest instructed Alban in the Christian faith, and Alban embraced Christ in his heart. But the Roman authorities heard that a Christian priest was hiding in Alban's house, and sent soldiers to make a thorough search.

Alban saw the soldiers coming, and immediately put the priest's long cloak round his own shoulders. He then gave himself up to the soldiers, in the place of his guest and teacher. The soldiers bound Alban in chains, and dragged him before the judge. When Alban was brought in, the judge was offering sacrifices to the pagan gods. The judge recognised Alban, and was furious that this respectable citizen had been so foolish as to surrender himself to the soldiers in place of the priest.

1.7 Alban's Trial

The judge ordered that Alban be forced to stand in front of the statues of pagan gods, where he had been offering sacrifices. 'Since you have chosen to conceal a sacrilegious rebel,' the judge pronounced, 'you shall suffer all the tortures due to him. Your only hope is to denounce that rebel's religion, and turn again to our gods.' Alban was unmoved by these threats. He calmly declared himself to be a Christian, and thus refused to worship the pagan gods.

'What is your family and race?' demanded the judge. 'How does my family concern you?' Alban replied; 'if you wish to know about my faith, let me repeat that I am a Christian, and follow the teachings of Jesus Christ.' 'I command you to tell me your name,' the judge insisted. 'My parents named me Alban, and I worship the true and living God, who created all things.' The judge was now furious. 'If you want to enjoy eternal life,' he shouted, 'offer a sacrifice at once to our great gods.' 'Your gods', Alban replied, 'have no power to help those who worship them, nor can they answer prayers.'

1.8 Alban's Execution

The judge ordered that Alban be flogged. 'Since words cannot move him,' the judge declared, 'let his heart be shaken by his wounds.' The judge stood and watched the beating. But, to the judge's horror, Alban did not flinch; and, with his face serene with spiritual joy, Alban continued to declare his allegiance to Christ. So the judge sentenced Alban to be beheaded at once. The soldiers led Alban out of the city gate towards the hill where he was to die.

The people of the city had heard what was happening and they had gathered along the route. When they saw Alban's radiant face, their hearts were filled with awe and wonder. One of the soldiers was so moved that he threw down his sword and fell at Alban's feet, begging to become a martyr also. The other soldiers could not bring themselves to arrest their comrade, who was allowed to follow Alban up the hill.

It was mid-summer, so the hill was robed in wild flowers of every colour. When they reached the summit Alban raised his eyes towards heaven in prayer; then he knelt down on the ground, laying bare his neck. The judge's executioners first beheaded Alban; and, as his blood spilt onto the ground, they beheaded the soldier who had fallen at his feet.

1.9 The End of Persecution and the Rise of Heresy

After the death of Alban many other Christians were executed throughout Britain, even as far west as Caerleon on the River Usk. Those who could escape the towns and cities without detection took refuge in woods and mountains, living in simple huts or caves. Eventually the persecution came to an end, and the Christians returned to their homes. They built shrines to the martyrs, and celebrated their festivals with renewed joy.

A few years later, Constantius, a man of exceptional kindness and courtesy who had ruled Gaul and Spain during the time of Diocletian, died during a visit to Britain. His son Constantine, who was with him, declared himself emperor of the whole Roman empire. Constantine's mother, Helena, who had been Constantius' concubine, was a devout Christian. So when her son arrived in Rome as emperor, she influenced him to make peace with all Christians. This did not, however, mark an end to the Church's troubles. Heresies of all kinds started to infect the Church from within, causing bitter divisions. And these various heresies even spread to this remote island.

1.10 Wars Between the British Nations

In the early years of the fifth century Rome came under increasing attack from the Goths. And in AD 410 , the Roman troops left Britain to defend Rome, taking with them all their equipment and also the strongest young men of this island. Thus Roman rule came to an end, almost 470 years after Julius Caesar landed. Britain now lay exposed to attack, lacking both weapons and soldiers trained in the art of war. Scots from the north-west and Picts from the north were able to cross the wall which the Romans had built, murdering the people on the south side and stealing their livestock.

On two occasions the Britons sent messages to Rome, appealing for help; and both times a legion arrived which drove back the enemies, inflicting heavy losses. But the Romans now told the Britons that they could no longer defend such a remote corner of the empire, and so the Britons must learn to fight for themselves. They pointed out it was not their lack of skill, but rather their weakness of will, which gave their enemies an advantage. The Picts and Scots heard that the Romans did not intend to return. So as soon as the last Roman troops had left, they renewed their attacks with even greater ferocity. And the southern Britons proved unable to resist. Many were killed, torn in pieces like lambs torn apart by wild beasts. Those who survived fled from their farms, and lived in the forests, struggling to survive by hunting.

1.11 Moral Corruption Amongst the British

By learning to hunt wild animals, the Britons gradually gained courage and became adept at wielding weapons of every kind. Eventually they felt strong enough to turn their weapons on their enemies. Making frequent sallies from the forests and mountains, they harassed the Picts and Scots who had taken over their farms, forcing them to flee northwards back to their own land. The Britons also fought the Irish pirates who had been plundering the west coast; and the Irish decided to stay at home for a period, until the military fervour of the British had abated. While they were fighting, the Britons frequently prayed to God, asking for divine help in their battles.

But once the Britons had defeated their enemies, they forgot God, and sought only material property and pleasure. Soon crime was rife throughout Britain. People lied and cheated; they stole each other's goods and livestock; and those who remained honest and generous became the targets of slander and even physical assault. Even the Christian priests were more frequently drunk than sober. When the Picts, Scots and Irish saw this corruption, they seized the opportunity to renew their attacks, displaying even greater ferocity and cruelty than before.

1.12 Vortigern's Invitation to the Angles and Saxons

As the attacks from the north became more fierce, and the Britons saw that their wickedness had made them too weak to defend themselves, one of the British chieftains, Vortigern, proposed that they seek the help of the Saxon people from across the sea. The leaders of the British people gathered to consider the proposal, and decided to accept it. Thus in the year of our Lord 449 a group of Angles and Saxons, at the invitation of Vortigern, arrived in Britain in three longships. The Britons gave them land on the eastern coast, on condition that they protect the country from attack.

But the real intention of the Angles and the Saxons was to conquer Britain for themselves. They began by marching north, where they quickly defeated the Picts and the Scots. They then sent a message back to their homeland, telling their people that the land was fertile and the Britons cowardly; they urged others to cross the sea and join them. Soon a much larger fleet arrived, carrying a massive army of seasoned warriors. The Angles and Saxons were now invincible. The Britons had no choice but to grant them huge tracts of land.

1.13 *Anglo-Saxon Ascendency*

Now the British people, who had invited the Angles and Saxons to their island as protectors, lived in fear of them. The first chieftains of the Angles and Saxons in Britain were Hengist and Horsa, who set about subduing the native people. Some brave Britons resisted, and Horsa was killed by them. The Angles now made an alliance with the Picts from the north, demanding that the Britons hand over a large portion of their livestock and annual harvest to them. The Britons refused. The Angles replied by renouncing their original treaty to protect the British people.

With the Picts the Angles now set about destroying the towns and villages of this island. From the east to the west both public and private buildings were burnt to the ground. Priests were slain at their altars, and families murdered in their homes. Nobody remained to bury the dead, since all who survived fled to the forests and mountains. Some eked out a miserable existence by hunting wild animals. Others became so desperate that they came out of the forests and begged the Angles for food; the Angles forced them to become slaves.

Part 2

Gregory and Augustine:
the Gospel in Kent

2.1 Gregory and the English Slaves

One day an eminent Christian scholar called Gregory was walking through the market-place in Rome, when he saw at one of the stalls a group of boys being sold as slaves. These boys had fair complexions, fine features and golden hair. Gregory was struck by their beauty, and asked from what country they came. 'They come from the island of Britain,' he was told, 'where all the people look like this.' He then asked whether the people of Britain were Christian, or whether they were still heathen. 'They are pagans,' came the reply. Gregory sighed with sadness that such bright and beautiful people should still live in spiritual darkness. 'What is the name of this race?' he asked. 'They are called Angles,' he was told. 'Not Angles, but angels,' he answered, 'for they have angelic faces. And from what province of Britain have they been brought?' 'From Deira,' he was told. 'That is appropriate. They shall indeed be rescued from *de ira* – from wrath – and be called to the peace of Christ. And what is the name of their king?' 'Aelle.' 'Then it is right that the people of that land should sing "Alleluia!".'

2.2. Gregory's Hopes and Augustine's Fears

Gregory immediately went to see the Pope, and offered to lead a group of preachers on a mission to Britain. The Pope refused because the people of Rome valued Gregory's presence among them so highly. But soon afterwards the Pope died, and Gregory was elected his successor. Gregory could not forget the young boys he had seen in the market-place; and so in the year of our Lord 596 he appointed a monk called Augustine, along with about forty of his brethren, to preach the word of God to the English nation. Augustine and his companions set off towards Britain with the Pope's fervent blessing. But after they had travelled some distance Augustine and his companions were seized with fear: the prospect of going to such a fierce and barbarous people, whose language was different from their own, appalled them. So they decided that Augustine should return to Rome, and beg Pope Gregory to recall them from this mission. Gregory refused Augustine's request, and instead wrote a letter of encouragement to the monks. 'My very dear sons,' he wrote, 'it is better not to undertake such a high enterprise, than to abandon it once it has begun. So with God's help you must complete the mission which you have started. Do not be deterred by the hardships of the journey, or by the dark warnings of future dangers. Be constant and determined. And be assured that the greater your labour, the greater will be the glory of your eternal reward.'

2.3 *Augustine's Arrival at Thanet*

In the year of our Lord 597 Augustine and his companions landed on the island of Thanet, off the coast of Kent. On the advice of Pope Gregory they had brought interpreters from the Frankish people. Augustine sent these interpreters to Ethelbert, the powerful king of Kent whose domains extended northwards right up to the River Humber. Through the interpreters Augustine told Ethelbert that he and his brethren had come from Rome, bearing wonderful news; and that all who received this news would enjoy eternal bliss in heaven, in the presence of the true and living God. The king responded by ordering Augustine and his monks to remain on the island where they had landed. He arranged that they should be given food and every material comfort, while he decided what action he should take. He already knew about the Christian faith, since his wife Bertha was Christian. She was from the Frankish royal house; and her parents had permitted the marriage only on condition that she should be free to practise her faith.

2.4 The Meeting of Augustine and Ethelbert

After Augustine and his brethren had been on the island of Thanet for some days, King Ethelbert came to see them. He refused to meet them inside any building, because he feared that they might possess magical powers – and there was an ancient superstition that magic was more powerful indoors. So he insisted that they meet in the open air. The monks approached the king carrying a silver cross and a picture of Jesus Christ on a wooden board. As they came near the king, they knelt down and sang a litany, praying both for themselves and for the English people whom they had come to serve. The king then commanded them to sit down, and the monks explained to him and his courtiers the rudiments of the Christian faith. When they had finished, the king said: 'Your doctrines and your promises are indeed wonderful. But they are new to me and my people so we cannot tell whether they are true. So we cannot immediately abandon our age-old religion, and adopt this religion which you offer. I can see that you are sincere, and you have travelled a long way in order to share your beliefs with us. In recognition of this we will not harm you, nor will we forbid you from preaching your religion. On the contrary, we will welcome you warmly, supplying you with food and shelter; and we will allow you to try and win new adherents to your faith from amongst our people.'

2.5 Community in Canterbury

Ethelbert gave Augustine and his brethren a large house in Canterbury, which was the capital city; and, as he had promised he supplied them with ample food and drink. When the monks walked into Canterbury they sang a hymn: 'We ask you, O Lord, in your mercy to turn your anger away from this city, and look with favour on its people.' As soon as they had settled in their house, they imitated the first Christians in Jerusalem. They met frequently to pray, they studied the teachings of the apostles as recorded in Holy Scripture, and they preached the gospel of Christ to anyone who would listen. Augustine and his companions now went on long journeys around Kent to tell people in remote villages and farms about Jesus Christ. Those who met them were struck by the holiness of their lives, and were enthralled by their message; and a growing number decided to embrace the Christian faith, and receive baptism. On the eastern side of the city of Canterbury stood an old church, built in honour of Saint Martin during the Roman occupation. Queen Bertha used to go there to pray, and now the monks began to worship there also. They invited the new Christians to join them, and soon the church was packed with people every morning and evening.

2.6 Etheldreda's Conversion and Augustine's Elevation

Eventually King Ethelbert himself was so impressed by the love which the monks showed for all people, and was convinced by their promise of eternal life to all who believe the gospel, that he asked to be baptised. His conversion convinced many others that they too should abandon their old religion and become Christian. Initially the king did not try to compel or coerce others to follow his example, but allowed people to weigh up this new religion for themselves. As Augustine frequently reiterated, conversion to Christianity must always be a matter of personal choice, made freely by each individual. But soon Ethelbert was showing special favours to other Christians. And he moved Augustine and his brethren to the finest house in Canterbury, second only to his palace in size and beauty. Augustine decided that the English people should now have their own bishop, and that he should fill this high office. So he travelled back to Arles, and asked the archbishop there to consecrate him. The archbishop agreed. Augustine then sent a letter to Pope Gregory, telling him of the success of his mission, and that he had become the first bishop of the English nation.

2.7 Pope Gregory's Letter on Bishops, Money and Worship

Augustine's letter to Pope Gregory also asked for advice on a wide variety of matters, including the functions of a bishop, the use of money, and forms of worship. In his reply Gregory gave these instructions: 'Regarding a bishop's duties, you should simply follow the guidance of Scripture, especially the letters of Paul to Timothy. The money which the bishop and clergy receive from the faithful should be divided into four. One part should go to the bishop himself to provide for his own needs and to enable him to give food to all who come to his house. The second part should go to the clergy, to provide for their needs. The third part should be given to the poor. And the fourth should pay for the construction and maintenance of church buildings.

'The bishops and clergy', Pope Gregory's letter continued, 'should never accumulate wealth, so they should give away any money they do not spend. They should live simply, and pray regularly. The bishop and clergy should use whatever forms of worship are most suitable for the people they are serving. They should study the forms of worship used elsewhere, selecting and adapting those parts which will uplift their own people. Forms of worship should not be loved for their own sake, but only for their spiritual value to the common people.'

2.8 Pope Gregory's Letter on Church Organisation

As the number of converts continued to grow, Augustine and his brethren found themselves unable to offer pastoral care and guidance to them. And they did not have enough sacred vessels for celebrating Mass. So in the year of our Lord 601 Augustine again wrote to Pope Gregory; and in this letter he asked the Pope to send more priests and sacred vessels, in order to reap the harvest which the monks had sown. Pope Gregory responded by sending several of his most able clergy and also a special mantle for Augustine to wear during worship as a sign of his spiritual authority. In addition the Pope sent instructions as to how the Church in England should be organised: 'Let the chief bishop for southern England reside in London; and in the future the bishop should be elected by a synod of the clergy. The bishop of London should in turn divide southern England into twelve dioceses, appointing a bishop to each. Choose one of your priests to become the chief bishop of northern England, and let him reside in York. The bishop of York should in turn divide northern England into twelve dioceses, appointing a bishop to each. During your lifetime, you shall be Bishop of London; and the bishop of York will be subject to your authority. But after your death London and York should be managed independently of one another. The bishops of southern and northern England should come together from time to time to discuss matters of doctrine; and at these meetings the bishop of London or the bishop of York should take precedence depending on their seniority of consecration.'

2.9 Pope Gregory's Letter on the Treatment of Ancient Religions

One of those sent by Pope Gregory, in response to Augustine's request for more priests, was an abbot called Mellitus. Gregory gave Mellitus a letter, concerning the way in which the traditional religion of the English people should be treated: 'After careful thought I have reached the conclusion that the old temples should be preserved. The idols inside the temples should be destroyed. But the buildings themselves should be sprinkled with holy water; and then Christian altars should be put where the idols stood, and relics of the saints sealed inside the altars. By turning their temples into churches, you will make it easier for the people to adopt the new faith: they will continue to come to their old places of worship, but will pray to the true and living God instead of their false gods. Preserve also their old festivals,' Pope Gregory's letter continued, 'giving new meaning to their traditional celebrations. For example, at those festivals when they used to sacrifice cattle to their gods, let them kill the same animals in order to hold a feast in honour of our saints. And as they enjoy the food, let them give thanks to God, the creator of all good things. If the people are allowed these worldly pleasures, they will be more inclined to enjoy the pleasures of the spirit. Do not try to eradicate their old errors at a single stroke; whoever wants to climb a mountain must go step by step.'

2.10 Pope Gregory's Letter on the Dangers of Pride

At the same time that he wrote to Mellitus, Pope Gregory also sent a letter to Augustine, warning him against personal pride: 'My very dear brother, I hear that through the power of Almighty God you have enjoyed great success amongst the English people. Let your emotions be a mixture of joy and fear: joy that through the efforts of you and your brethren the English people are being driven towards the love of God; and fear that your frail mind becomes proud of these achievements. Your mission to the English nation has made you famous, and your name is held in the highest public esteem. Yet beware of taking pleasure in this; your only pleasure should be in the knowledge that your name is written in heaven. You have been chosen by God to preach his gospel and to perform miracles in his service. Others are chosen by God to undertake more humble and less conspicuous tasks. All those who obey God's will are equal in his sight. So in all your outward actions examine carefully your inner motives, judging them by the highest standards. You will frequently find that your motives are tainted with impurity; let the knowledge of this crush any temptation towards pride that may rise in your heart.'

2.11 Pope Gregory's Letter on Christian Kings

Pope Gregory recognised that Augustine's mission to the English people had gained great strength from the support of King Ethelbert. So he sent the king various gifts as tokens of gratitude, and also a letter: 'The reason why Almighty God raises good men to be rulers of nations is that through these men he may bless the common people. This is undoubtedly true of the English nation: you have been anointed by God as king of the English in order that the people of England may hear the gospel of Christ. Make the conversion of the English people your first concern. Raise the moral standards of your subjects by the example of your own moral purity. Encourage your subjects to be gentle and generous to one another, and warn them against violence and greed. Remember that the emperor Constantine, by submitting to Christ himself, turned the entire Roman empire away from the worship of idols, towards the worship of the true and living God. As a result his reputation exceeds that of all his predecessors. You are called to be the Constantine of the English; and, by bringing your people to the Christian faith, you will outshine all earlier English kings. Work closely with Bishop Augustine. Listen to his advice without resentment, and follow it without hesitation. Support all his efforts with the strength God has given you.'

2.12 Augustine's First Meeting with the British Christians

Augustine, with the help of King Ethelbert, called a meeting with the Christian leaders in other parts of Britain. The conference was held at a place which is now known by the English as Augustine's Oak, on the western side of Britain. Augustine urged the British Christians to accept him as their brother, and thus become part of the universal Church. And he proposed that as brothers they could work together in preaching the gospel to the heathen. The British Christians did not keep Easter at the correct date; and many of their other customs were contrary to the practice of the universal Church. Augustine thus urged them to observe the Roman date of Easter. The discussion was long and at times heated. They stopped frequently to pray for guidance; and Augustine often accused the British of being stubborn and narrow-minded. Eventually the British acknowledged that Augustine was sincere in his faith, and that much of what he said was true. But they concluded that they could not abandon their ancient religious customs without the consent and approval of their own people. So they asked that a second and fuller conference be arranged. Augustine agreed.

2.13 Augustine's Second Meeting with the British Christians

The British Christians now went to visit a hermit who was renowned for his wisdom and holiness. They asked the hermit whether they should abandon their ancient religious customs, and accept Augustine as their leader. 'If he is a man of God, follow him,' the hermit replied. 'But how can we tell whether he is a man of God?' 'A man of God is gentle and humble, like Christ himself. If Augustine is gentle and humble, he is truly a disciple of Christ. If he is arrogant and proud, he is not a man of God, and you should not listen to him.' 'But how can we tell even this?' they asked. 'Arrange that Augustine and his followers arrive first at the place chosen for the conference. If he rises from his chair to greet you, then you can be sure that he is a servant of Christ. But if he ignores you and does not rise, do not accept him as your leader.' The British Christians did as the hermit suggested; and as they arrived at the conference, Augustine did not rise to greet them. The British Christians accused him of arrogance and pride. The conference then became increasingly angry. Finally Augustine said: 'There are many points at which your customs differ from those of the universal Church. Nevertheless, if you will agree with me on three points, I will tolerate all your other customs. First, you must celebrate Easter at the correct date; secondly, you must perform baptism according to the rites of the Church in Rome; and thirdly, you must join with me in preaching the word of God to the English.' The British Christians refused these demands, and declared that they would not accept him as their bishop. 'If he will not rise to greet us now,' they said to one another, 'he would have even less regard for us once we submitted to his authority.'

Part 3

Paulinus and Edwin:
the Gospel in York

3.1 New Bishops and Augustine's Death

In the year of our Lord 604 Augustine consecrated two bishops, Mellitus and Justus, both of whom had come from Rome when Augustine had appealed to Pope Gregory for more priests. Mellitus was appointed to the province of the East Saxons, which lies to the north of the River Thames, and is bounded on the east by the sea. Its capital is London, which is a trading port with ships coming from across the world. The province fell within King Ethelbert's domain, and he had appointed his nephew Sabert to govern it. Ethelbert ordered that a church be built in London for Mellitus and his successors, dedicated to the apostle Paul. Justus was appointed to the city of Rochester, to the west of Canterbury. Ethelbert built there a church dedicated to the apostle Andrew; and he later gave land to provide an income for Justus and his successors. Augustine died later that year. The church in Canterbury, dedicated to the apostles Peter and Paul, had not yet been completed; so Augustine was buried in the north porch. Before he died Augustine consecrated Lawrence as his successor, one of Augustine's original companions. Lawrence made great efforts to persuade the British Christians to accept his authority; and he also wrote to the Scottish Christians with the same appeal. But both the Britons and the Scots remained stubbornly independent.

3.2 Setback Under Eadbald

In the year of our Lord 616 King Ethelbert died, after reigning for fifty-six years. He was buried beside his devout wife Bertha, who had died previously, in the porch of the great church he had built in Canterbury. His son Eadbald, who acceded to the throne, had always treated the Christian faith with contempt; and now he was king he indulged his immoral passions. Under Ethelbert many people in the kingdom, who secretly despised Christian teaching, had restrained themselves, for fear of incurring the king's wrath. But Eadbald's wicked behaviour prompted them to throw aside their inhibitions, and commit every kind of sexual sin. Soon afterwards, Sabert, who had governed the East Saxons on Ethelbert's behalf, also died. And his three sons proved even worse than Eadbald. A few days after their accession, they marched into the church in London while Bishop Mellitus was offering Mass and demanded to drink the consecrated wine. Mellitus refused, saying that only those who had been baptised could have the bread and wine. The three sons became angry, but Mellitus remained adamant. Finally they threw him out of the church, shouting that he and his followers should leave the province.

3.3 Eadbald's Conversion

After his expulsion from his church in London, Mellitus went to Kent, to consult with his fellow bishops Lawrence and Justus as to what they should do. They decided that they should abandon the mission to Britain. 'It is better for us to serve God in freedom elsewhere,' they said, 'than to remain here among people who have rejected the Christ.' Mellitus and Justus left immediately, with Lawrence to follow soon afterwards. On the night before he was due to go, Lawrence ordered that his bed be placed inside the church in Canterbury. For many hours he prayed for the Church in Britain, and then finally fell asleep. In a dream the apostle Peter came to him, demanding why he was running away from the flock entrusted to his care. 'Have you forgotten my example?' Peter asked. 'For the sake of those whom Christ entrusted to me, I endured imprisonment, beatings, and finally death by crucifixion.' When he awoke Lawrence found that there were marks of a whip on his back. That morning Lawrence went to King Eadbald, told him of his dream and showed him the marks. Eadbald was moved to tears by what he heard and saw; and he fell on his knees, begging Lawrence to baptise him. Later that day the king sent a message to Mellitus and Justus, urging them to return. The people of Rochester were delighted to see their bishop Justus again. But the people of London, under the three wicked sons of Sabert, again drove Mellitus out of their city.

3.4 The Arrival of Paulinus in York

Lawrence died soon after his dream, and Mellitus was elected to the bishopric of Canterbury. By now Canterbury was regarded as the senior English church. In 624 Mellitus died, and Justus was asked to move from Rochester to Canterbury. At this time the Northumbrian people, living north of the Humber, were ruled by a man called Edwin, whose castle was at York. He sent an embassy of nobles to Kent, to ask whether Eadbald would give his sister Ethelberga in marriage to him. After much hesitation Eadbald agreed, on condition that Ethelberga and her servants would be free to practice the Christian faith. Edwin not only accepted this condition, but undertook to study Christianity himself; and if he and his advisors came to the conclusion that it was superior to his pagan religion, he would adopt it. Justus appointed Paulinus, who had come to Britain with him, as Ethelberga's chaplain; he also consecrated Paulinus as bishop to the Northumbrians. Paulinus was a tall, thin man, with a slight stoop; his hair was black, and his nose hooked. As soon as Ethelberga and Paulinus arrived in Northumbria, Edwin, true to his word, asked Paulinus to instruct him in the Christian faith.

3.5 Edwin's Narrow Escape

A year after the marriage of Edwin and Ethelberga, the king of the West Saxons sent an assassin to kill Edwin; he then intended to invade Northumbria and add it to his own kingdom. The assassin had a double-edged dagger soaked in poison, so that if the wound was not fatal, the poison would complete his work. He arrived at the royal palace, by the River Derwent, on Easter Day. He told the palace officials that he had a message from his king to give to Edwin. As he approached Edwin's throne, he suddenly took the dagger from beneath his clothes, and lunged at Edwin. The king's closest advisor, who was standing beside the throne, threw himself at the dagger, to protect his master. Nonetheless the dagger went through the advisor's body, and wounded Edwin. That night, as Edwin lay on his bed fighting for his life, Paulinus came to him, and told him that Ethelberga had safely delivered a baby daughter, Eanfled. Edwin was overjoyed at the news, and Paulinus sang a hymn of praise to God. Edwin made a promise that, if God saved his life, he would submit to Christ; and, as a pledge, he gave his daughter to Paulinus to be consecrated to Christ. Thus on the feast of Pentecost the small child became the first Northumbrian to receive baptism. In the meantime Edwin recovered. He immediately summoned his army and attacked the West Saxons. He won a glorious victory. On returning home he asked Paulinus to continue instructing him in the faith.

3.6 The Chief Priest's Advice

After receiving further instruction from Paulinus, Edwin was convinced that he should accept the faith which Paulinus taught. But since as king his conversion would affect all his subjects, he decided to discuss the matter with his advisers and friends; indeed he hoped that they too would become Christian, and that in due course his entire kingdom would follow. Thus Edwin convened a council at his castle in York, and asked each of his advisers in turn their view of this strange new religion. Coifi, the chief priest of the old religion, replied first: 'I wish to give the most careful consideration to the Christian faith. I must honestly admit that in my experience, our old religion seems virtually useless. None of your subjects has been more devoted to the service of our gods than myself. Yet I have not benefitted at all from this devotion. There are many others in your kingdom who are less devoted and zealous in serving the gods; yet you have showered honours and wealth upon them, and they have been far more successful in their various activities than I have. If the gods had any power, they would surely have favoured me over them. So if you decide that this new religion is better than the old, we should not hesitate to accept it.'

3.7   A Pagan's Words of Wisdom

Another of Edwin's advisers indicated his agreement with Coifi's views, and added his own insights: 'When we compare our present life on earth with that time of which we have no knowledge, it seems to be like the swift flight of a single sparrow through the banqueting-hall, when you and your nobles are sitting at dinner on a cold winter's day. Inside the hall a fire is burning; outside the wind is howling and the snow is falling. The sparrow darts in through one door and out through another. For a few moments he is safe and warm; but then he goes back into the cold, harsh storms. In the same way each of us appears on this earth for a little while; but we know nothing of what went before, or what comes after. Thus if the Christian faith gives us greater knowledge of this mystery, we should accept it.' Edwin and his other advisers were deeply impressed by these wise words; and Coifi, the chief priest of the old religion, asked if Paulinus could instruct them all in the new religion.

3.8 The Baptism of Edwin by Paulinus

Paulinus explained the Christian faith to Edwin's advisers in great detail. When he had finished, Coifi, the chief priest, rose to speak: 'For a long time I have been aware that our old religion is nonsense. The more diligently I have sought the truth within it, the less I have found. I now publicly declare that this new religion clearly reveals truths that will bring us great happiness, both in the present life and after death. Therefore I recommend that the idols we have worshipped be destroyed, and that our temples be used to worship the God of whom Paulinus speaks.' At these words Edwin finally decided to embrace Christianity. Coifi immediately asked the king for a stallion, so he could ride round the kingdom destroying the pagan idols. When the people saw the chief priest galloping from temple to temple, with a spear in his hand, smashing every idol he could find, they thought he had gone mad. In the meantime Edwin ordered a church to be built near his castle at York. It was erected at great speed out of timber; and there on Easter Day 627 Edwin, and all the nobility of his kingdom, along with many humbler people, were baptised by Paulinus.

3.9 Edwin's Death and Paulinus' Retreat

In the year of our Lord 632, six years after he had received baptism, Edwin's kingdom of Northumbria was attacked by heathen warriors from Mercia, led by Penda, in alliance with the king of Wales. In a fierce battle near Doncaster Edwin was killed, and his army destroyed. Penda and his troops roamed Northumbria, destroying churches and killing all people of

Anglo-Saxon descent. Finally they arrived in York, carrying Edwin's head on the end of a spear; and they put the head on the altar of the church which Edwin had built. In the meantime Paulinus had taken Ethelburga, Edwin's queen, back to Kent, travelling by sea to avoid Penda's murderous soldiers. Paulinus left a young deacon called James to preserve the Christian faith in Northumbria. James was an expert in church music, and travelled from place to place encouraging the Christians by teaching them to sing hymns. Edwin's kingdom was now divided into two: Deira in the south, centred on York, and Bernicia in the north. The men who became kings were both relatives of Edwin, and had been instructed in the Christian faith; but as soon as they gained power, they both rejected the gospel, and began to indulge their immoral and wicked passions.

Part 4

Columba, Aidan and Oswald: the Gospel in Northumbria

4.1 Columba's Community and Oswald's Victory

In the year of our Lord 565 a priest and abbot called Columba came from Ireland to Britain. He and the other Irish monks who accompanied him settled on the small island of Iona. From there he travelled many times to the Picts who live to the north side of the Grampians, a range of steep and desolate mountains. He preached the gospel to them, and won many converts. He died on Iona in the year AD 597. Some years later, when Edwin was king of Northumbria, Edwin's nephew Oswald lived in Iona, learning the Christian faith. When after Edwin's death Northumbria was ruled by murderous heathen, Oswald decided to raise an army and bring Northumbria back under Christian rule. As he arrived at the northern border of Northumbria, near Hexham, he saw across a valley a vast horde of warriors ready to fight. He set up a large wooden cross on the top of a hill overlooking the valley, and knelt down to seek God's help in the coming battle. Then he shouted to his troops: 'Let us all kneel together, praying that God will give us strength to win back our nation. God knows that our cause is just.' The entire army knelt down, and joined their leader in prayer. The following morning as dawn was breaking Oswald led his troops towards the enemy, and achieved the victory which their faith deserved.

4.2 Aidan's Advice on Evangelism

As soon as he became king of Northumbria, Oswald decided to ask the monks in Iona to send one of their number to preach the gospel amongst his people. Initially they sent a man who was very austere. The people refused to listen to him; and after some time he returned to Iona, complaining that the people of Northumbria were too obstinate and barbarous in temperament to learn the Christian faith. The abbot called all the monks together, to decide what to do. The monks expressed their deep sadness at the failure of their companion to win converts; but they still wanted to work for the salvation of King Oswald's subjects. One of the brethren, called Aidan, addressed the monk whose efforts had been unsuccessful: 'It seems to me that you were too severe with your ignorant hearers. Like the first apostles, you should have begun by giving them the milk of simple teaching, gradually nourishing their souls until they were ready to receive the strong meat of Christian doctrine.' As Aidan spoke the faces and eyes of all the monks turned to him, and they realised that he was perfectly suited to this subtle task. So they immediately laid hands on him, and the following day he set off towards Northumbria.

4.3 Aidan's Practice of Evangelism

King Oswald's castle stood at the top of a rocky hill, on the Northumbrian coast. A short distance out to sea lies the island of Lindisfarne, which at low tide can be reached on foot across a bank of sand. When Aidan arrived he asked the king to let him form a community of monks on the island, like the community at Iona. Oswald happily agreed. Aidan had no knowledge of the English language which Oswald and his nobles spoke. But since Oswald had learnt Aidan's language during his stay at Iona, he initially acted as interpreter; and he also taught English to Aidan, who proved an eager and capable pupil. Aidan preached the gospel with such fluency and joy that young men began flocking to join him at Lindisfarne. There he trained them in the art of Christian fellowship and prayer. Then he began to tour the remote regions of Oswald's kingdom. He always travelled on foot, so he could talk to people on his journeys. He was utterly indifferent to people's social standing, speaking as eagerly about Christ to the humble peasants as to the wealthy lords.

4.4 *Aidan's Way of Life*

Since Aidan toured Northumbria on foot, he was unable to carry the Scriptures with him. So he learnt the New Testament and the Psalms by heart; and each day at the appointed times he would recite a psalm and a passage of Scripture to himself. In this way he maintained the monastic discipline. He dressed in simple woollen cloth, and ate whatever food was offered to him. Whenever a rich man gave him some precious object as a token of appreciation, he either handed it on to the poor, or used it to buy slaves their freedom. Many of these former slaves joined his community at Lindisfarne, and he trained them to preach the gospel. If Aidan saw wealthy or powerful people do wrong, he was outspoken in reprimanding them; he never kept silent out of respect for rank or fear of reprisal. But he much preferred to encourage people in the good they were doing. Whenever he observed someone being kind and generous to others, he was lavish in his praise; and if that person was not already a Christian, he taught them to recognise Christ as the author of their loving impulses.

4.5 *Oswald's Generosity*

Oswald looked to Aidan for advice on every kind of matter, both private and public. And with Aidan's help Oswald ruled his kingdom according to the highest standards of justice and honesty. As a result his people lived in peace and harmony. In particular within the borders of Northumbria were members of all four nations which inhabit this island, British, Pictish, Scottish and English; and under Oswald they came to regard each other as friends. Despite the great power he wielded, Oswald always remained humble and generous to the poor. One Easter Day he and Aidan were dining together. A silver dish of rich food was brought in; and just as Aidan was raising his hand to bless the food, a servant came in to say that there was a great crowd of poor families outside the castle begging for alms. At once Oswald ordered that his own food be taken out to them; and that the silver dish be broken up, so that a piece could be given to each family. This exemplary king extended his rule southwards, bringing Deira and Bernicia back into unity, as they had been under his uncle King Edwin.

4.6 Oswald's Death and Successors

Oswald reigned over Northumbria for only nine years. In 642 Penda led an army of Mercian warriors against the Northumbrian people. Oswald gathered his troops and marched towards the Mercians. They met at Oswestry, on 5 August. After a fierce battle the Northumbrian soldiers were routed, and Oswald himself killed. After Oswald's death, his younger brother Oswy secured power in the northern province of Bernicia; and some time later his cousin Oswin gained power in Deira. The Mercians continued to attack both provinces from the south; and members of Oswy's own family rebelled against him. Oswin was a tall, handsome man, who was always pleasant in speech and courteous in manner. He possessed natural authority, so that he was always treated with respect. He was generous and kind to all he met, high and low alike, showing concern for both their material and their spiritual needs. And, amongst his many virtues, the most striking was humility –

which is rarely to be found in rulers. Inevitably he warmed towards Aidan, and wanted to support Aidan in his Christian mission.

4.7 Oswin's Gift to Aidan

A single incident reveals both Oswin's love for Aidan and his astonishing humility. Oswin gave Aidan one of his finest horses, so that Aidan could ride whenever he had to cross a river or respond to an urgent call. Soon afterwards Aidan met a beggar, who asked him for alms. Aidan immediately gave the beggar his horse. Oswin heard about this; and the next time Aidan was visiting his castle, just as they were going to dine, Oswin said: 'Why did you give away one of the royal horses? As you know, we have many less valuable horses which would have been good enough for beggars. Surely you should have kept the horse which I personally had selected for you?' Aidan answered Oswald with a question of his own: 'Are you saying that the child of a mare is more valuable than a child of God?' After they reached the dining-hall Aidan sat down at the table. But Oswin, who had come in from hunting, stood in front of the fire, warming himself. Oswin said nothing for a few moments, reflecting on Aidan's words. Then suddenly he unbuckled his sword, handing it to a servant, and threw himself at Aidan's feet. 'Please forgive me,' he pleaded; 'I will never refer to this matter again. Nor will I ever ask how much of God's riches you give away to his children.'

4.8 Oswin's Murder by Oswy

Although at first Oswy in Bernicia and Oswin in Deira lived in peace, they soon became suspicious of one another's intentions, and accused one another of evil plots. Eventually they raised armies against one another, and met near the village of

Catterick. Oswin realised that his forces were far weaker than those of Oswy. So rather than risk a battle, he retreated and sent his troops back to their homes. He himself hid in the house of a nobleman named Hunwald, whom he regarded as his closest friend. But Hunwald proved a traitor, sending a message to Oswy of Oswin's whereabouts. Oswy promptly despatched a group of soldiers, who murdered Oswin in cold blood. When the people of both Bernicia and Deira heard of Oswy's crime, they were utterly revolted. And Oswy himself became so ashamed of what he had done that he built a monastery at the site of the murder, where prayers were offered daily both for himself and for his victim.

4.9 Aidan's Death

After sixteen years in Northumbria, touring its remote villages and farms to bring the good news of Christ, Aidan became too old and weary to continue. King Oswy, who now occupied the castle where Oswald had lived, built for Aidan a small wooden church near the castle; and next to the church he erected a simple hut where Aidan could live. During the day Aidan often stood leaning against one of the church's buttresses, where he could easily be seen; passers-by often came across to talk and pray with him. He was in this position when, on the last day of August in the year of our Lord 651, he quietly breathed his last. Aidan's body was then taken over to Lindisfarne and buried in the monks' cemetery. The brethren at Lindisfarne sent word to Iona that their beloved abbot had died; and the community at Iona sent a monk called Finan to take his place. Some years later, Penda, the king of Mercia, came and attacked the royal castle, and burnt the church and hut where Aidan had spent his final months on earth. But the wooden buttress, on which Aidan was leaning at the moment of death, was preserved from the flames. The local people, who had loved Aidan dearly, lifted the buttress from the ashes;

and in due course they put it inside another church, as a memorial of Aidan. Since that time so many people have cut chips from the buttress, believing that these chips would have miraculous properties, that very little of the buttress remains.

Part 5

Felix, Fursey and Etheldreda: the Gospel in East Anglia

5.1 Sigbert's Invitation to Felix

The first king of the East Angles to receive baptism was Redwald. He visited Kent, and was deeply impressed by the Christian religion which he saw practised there. But when he returned home his wife and various advisers urged him to abandon his new faith. In the face of this opposition he tried to compromise by building a temple with two altars, one dedicated to Christ and the other to the pagan gods. Redwald's son, called Earpwald, was a friend of Edwin, the king of Northumbria. Redwald died at about the time that Edwin and his nobles became Christian; and Edwin then persuaded Earpwald to embrace fully the Christian religion. But Earpwald failed to convince his nobles and people to follow his example; and shortly afterwards a pagan priest murdered him. For three years there was chaos throughout the land, until Earpwald's younger brother Sigbert secured the throne. Sigbert had himself converted to Christianity in France. He met there a young monk called Felix, who felt called to preach the gospel to the East Angles. So when Sigbert became king of the East Angles he invited Felix to lead a mission to his subjects. For seventeen years Felix lived at Dunwich, on the coast, where he established a monastery. And he and his monks went out from there, visiting every village and homestead in the kingdom and telling the people about Christ. They reaped a rich harvest of believers.

5.2 Fursey's Early Life

Felix and his companions concentrated their efforts mainly in the southern part of Sigbert's kingdom. The mission to the northern part was led by a remarkable man from Ireland called Fursey. He came from a noble family, but from an early age adopted a monastic way of life, devoting himself to prayer, eating simple food and wearing the rough clothes of a peasant. When he reached adulthood he built himself a hut in a remote forest in order to worship God and study the Scriptures in solitude. After several years he fell ill with a fever; and one night during this illness he had an astonishing vision. He left his body and was carried by an angel to a great height. The angel ordered him to look down to the world; and below him he saw a dark valley in which four fires were burning. He asked the angels to explain these fires. 'The first is Falsehood,' replied the angel, 'which is the source of all evil. The second is Envy, which occurs when people put the love of material wealth before the love of God. The third is Discord, which occurs when people fail to consider the needs and feelings of their neighbours. And the fourth is Cruelty, when people injure others in the pursuit of material gain.' The four fires gradually spread, until eventually they merged into one great conflagration that filled the entire valley.

5.3 Fursey's Vision

Fursey in his vision felt the flames of Falsehood, Envy, Discord and Cruelty leap up towards him, and he felt their searing heat. He screamed to the angel who had carried him to this great height, begging to be saved. 'Do not be afraid,' the angel replied; 'the fires of sin are also the fires which refine and purify the soul. These fires are burning away your evil desires.' Then out of the flames arose the image of a man whom he recognised; he remembered visiting him as he lay dying, and receiving from him the gift of a coat. Fursey heard a voice accusing him of taking advantage of the man's condition, and thus stealing the coat. 'I accepted the gift', Fursey answered, 'in order to help save his soul.' The angel spoke again to Fursey: 'God is calling you no longer to be a hermit, but to go out among the people, and turn the flames of sin into the refining fire which purifies souls. You will be subject to many other slanders and false accusations, like the one made against you by the dead man. This is the fate of all true disciples of Christ.' The angel now took Fursey's soul back to his body, which in the meantime had recovered from the fever. The next morning Fursey left his hut in the forest; and for the next few years he walked from place to place throughout Ireland, preaching the gospel of Christ.

5.4 Fursey's Arrival at Burgh Castle

Fursey was such an inspiring preacher that soon crowds were flocking to hear him wherever he went. At first he was pleased at this success; but eventually he grew weary of constantly being surrounded by people. So he walked to the east coast of Ireland, built a small boat, and set sail across the sea. The winds and currents took his boat around the coast of Britain, and then blew him ashore at the mouth of the River Yare, in the province of the East Angles. There he found the ruins of a Roman fort, Burgh Castle, where for a period he lived again as a hermit. But Sigbert, the devout king of the East Angles, heard of Fursey's arrival. He urged Fursey to preach the gospel among his subjects; and to turn the fort into a monastery, where he could train young men also to become preachers. Fursey reluctantly agreed, and began to tour the northern part of Sigbert's kingdom, winning large numbers of souls for Christ. And the Roman fort soon filled with men studying the Scriptures. One of these men became a close friend to Fursey, and it was to him that Fursey related his vision. This man recalled many years later that the day on which he spoke was cold and frosty; yet Fursey sweated profusely, as he remembered the heat of the fires.

5.5 King Sigbert's Monastic Vocation

Under the influence of both Felix and Fursey, King Sigbert grew increasingly ardent in his faith. Eventually he decided to entrust the rule of the East Angles to a relative called Egric, who already governed part of the territory, and to retire to Felix's monastery at Dunwich. There he devoted himself to prayer. Some years later the Mercian warriors, led by King Penda, attacked the East Angles. Egric, who had little experience in warfare, pleaded with Sigbert to come and lead the East Anglian troops into battle. Sigbert refused, saying that he had taken monastic vows which prohibited him from carrying arms. But, despite Sigbert's protest, Egric's men dragged him from the monastery to the battle field, believing that the East Anglian soldiers would fight more bravely if they could merely see their former commander nearby. Sigbert stood and watched the battle. Egric was killed, along with most of his army; and the few survivors fled into the forest. Then a group of Penda's officers rode up to Sigbert, and murdered him.

5.6 Etheldreda's Marriage

After ransacking many of the churches built by Felix and Fursey, Penda and his soldiers rode back to Mercia; and Anna, cousin to Sigbert, became king. Anna's eldest daughter Etheldreda married Egfrid, who had become king of Northumbria. They lived together for twelve years, but throughout that time Etheldreda refused to have intercourse with him, saying that she wished to devote herself wholly to Christ. Egfrid offered her vast estates and great wealth if she would consummate the marriage, but she remained adamant. Eventually Etheldreda asked to be released from the union, in order to live in a convent. Egfrid was furious at this request, and tried to confine her in his castle. One night she managed to escape, and fled to the convent at Coldingham, where Egfrid's aunt, called Ebba, was abbess. When Egfrid learnt where his wife had gone, he rode with a group of soldiers to Coldingham to fetch her back. But seeing Egfrid on the horizon, Etheldreda and two nuns slipped out of the convent into the forest. They walked southwards for many weeks until at last they reached Etheldreda's native country, where she felt safe.

5.7 Etheldreda's Convent at Ely

On the western side of the kingdom of the East Angles lies the island of Ely, deriving its name from the vast quantity of eels caught in the fens all around it. Before her marriage to Egfrid she had frequently visited this secluded place in order to pray; and now she set about establishing a convent there. When word spread of this new venture, other devout women flocked to join her, so soon the island was filled with the sound of hymns and prayers. Etheldreda inspired her sisters through the simplicity and austerity of her life. She never wore linen, but only rough wool. She bathed every day in cold water, except on the great festivals of Easter, Pentecost and Epiphany when she allowed herself warm water. She ate only one meal a day, praying in silence. Her most striking attribute was the gift of prophecy: she was able to predict events with great accuracy long before they occurred. Not long after arriving at Ely she prophesied that the plague would kill her after she had been on the island for seven years; and she was proved correct. Her younger sister Sexburga, who had been married to the king of Kent, came to Ely to take her place as abbess. Sexburga and a group of nuns took a boat to the ruined Roman town of Grantchester, where they found a beautiful sarcophagus. They brought it back to Ely and placed it in the church; then with great ceremony they placed Etheldreda's body within it.

Part 6

Cedd, Earconwald and Ethelburga: the Gospel in Essex

6.1 *Sigbert's Conversion by Oswy*

Although the East Saxons had originally rejected the Christian faith and expelled Bishop Mellitus, they eventually embraced Christ through the example and preaching of a monk from Northumbria called Cedd. Cedd was invited to come to the East Saxons by their king, named Sigbert – not the Sigbert who ruled the East Angles. Sigbert was a friend of Oswy, king of Northumbria, and often used to visit Oswy's castle. Oswy and Sigbert discussed religious matters in great depth. Oswy argued that the ancient gods which Sigbert and his people worshipped in their temples were merely blocks of wood and stone, with no greater value than the wood thrown onto a fire or the stone used in building walls. Oswy went on to explain that the true God is invisible to human eyes, yet possesses infinite power. This God has existed since before time began, and will exist after time is complete; and is the creator of the entire universe. He rules the world with justice, so that after death the wicked are punished and the good are rewarded. After many discussions comparing the ancient gods with the Christian God, Oswy persuaded Sigbert and his advisers to convert to the new religion. They were baptised at a village called Walton, so named because it stands close to the wall which the Romans built to keep out the Picts and Scots. The ceremony was performed by Finan, Aidan's successor at Lindisfarne.

6.2 Cedd's Arrival at Othona Castle

After his baptism in Northumbria, in which he became a citizen of the heavenly kingdom, Sigbert returned to his earthly kingdom. But before he left Northumbria, he asked King Oswy to send a Christian preacher to spread the gospel of Christ amongst the East Saxons. At this time Cedd, who had trained at Lindisfarne, was touring the kingdom of Mercia, preaching to the Middle Angles who had settled there. Oswy decided that Cedd was the ideal man to lead a mission to the East Saxons; so he sent a message to him, summoning him back to Northumbria. Cedd went to Lindisfarne, where he discussed his new task with Finan; he also spent many days and nights praying to God for strength and wisdom, that he might convey the truth revealed by Christ in a manner acceptable to the East Saxon people. Cedd then sailed down the east coast of Britain until he arrived at the old Roman fort of Othona. He built for himself a small hut and church within the walls of the fort, and began to pray for the conversion of the East Saxons. Soon local people began visiting him, and he taught them about Christ. Whenever an unmarried young man converted to Christianity, Cedd invited him to remain at Othona, in order to train as a preacher. Gradually he established a large monastery, which sent out men across the kingdom. Once he felt confident that the community at Othona was firmly rooted, Cedd sailed onwards to Tilbury, where he set up another monastery on the same lines. In this way all of King Sigbert's subjects heard the gospel.

6.3 Cedd's Defeat of Evil

While he was leading the mission to the East Saxons, Cedd, a man of inexhaustible energy, frequently returned to the kingdom of Northumbria, in order to preach the gospel to his own people. During one of his visits Ethelwald, who governed the province of Deira, asked Cedd to found a monastery there.

Ethelwald explained that he wanted a place where he himself could come for spiritual refreshment, and where a group of monks would pray daily for God's guidance on him in his work. This plan appealed to Cedd; and he chose Lastingham, a remote site in the Pennine hills which was currently being used as a hideout for thieves and murderers. Ethelwald was surprised at Cedd's choice; but, at Cedd's insistence, he ordered his soldiers to drive the criminals away. Cedd then stayed alone at the site throughout the season of Lent, purifying it through constant prayer and fasting. He ate each day only one slice of bread, an egg and a cup of watered milk. At Easter he invited a small group of other monks to join him; and after their Easter celebrations, they built a chapel and some huts. Once the chapel was complete Ethelwald came to visit. And he understood at once the value of the site: by defeating the evil influence of the criminals, Cedd had established it as a place of great spiritual power. In the following years Ethelwald fulfilled his intention of frequently coming to stay there; and his work as governor of Deira was greatly enhanced by the prayers of the monks. Cedd himself went back to the East Saxons. But many years later Cedd returned to this Pennine monastery. And in 659 while he was there, the plague swept through the region and killed him.

6.4 Earconwald, the Sick Healer

In 665, six years after the death of Cedd, Sigbert died, and Sebbi became king of the East Saxons. And a few years later Theodore, the new archbishop of Canterbury, appointed Earconwald as bishop of the East Saxons. Earconwald was a man of exceptional holiness, who throughout his life suffered from poor health. By the time he became bishop he was unable to walk or ride; so he had to travel round the land of the East Saxons lying down in straw, in a cart pulled by a horse. Earconwald built two monasteries, which soon became famous for their strict discipline and fervent prayer. The first was for men, and was situated on the banks of the River Thames at Chertsey. Earconwald regarded this as his home, and returned there whenever his duties as a bishop permitted. Earconwald's second monastery was for men and women, and was situated at Barking, in the heart of the land of the East Saxons. The abbess of this community was Earconwald's sister, called Ethelburga, who was tireless in caring for the spiritual and material needs of the monks and nuns in her charge. Both she and Earconwald acquired a reputation for healing people who were sick in body or soul. They exercised this ministry through the power of their prayers and the holiness of their lives. When Earconwald was travelling, sick people often came at night to take the straw from his cart, believing that they could be cured by lying on it themselves.

6.5 Ethelburga and the Plague

One summer the plague swept through the land of the East Saxons. Earconwald travelled to as many places as he could manage, praying for those who were sick. He himself did not catch the disease, and many were saved by his prayers. At Barking the plague attacked the men's part of the monastery; but for many months the women were spared, enabling them to pray night and day for the sick and bereaved. But Ethelburga told her nuns that in due course the plague would reach their part; and she asked them where they wished to be buried. The nuns could not decide, and prayed for guidance. Their prayers were answered one night just before dawn. As usual they had gathered in their chapel to sing God's praises. Then Ethelburga asked them to follow her out to the cemetery where the monks who had died of the plague were buried. The abbess led the nuns in prayer for the monks' souls. As she did so, the sun began to rise on the eastern horizon. The air was so clear that the sun shone even more brightly than it does at noon; and its rays bathed the south side of their chapel in a warm orange light.

The nuns knew at once that this is where they should be buried. The following day the plague struck the women's part of the monastery; and soon the south side of their chapel was filled with nuns' graves.

6.6 Holy Dying at Barking

A young boy whose parents had died in the plague was brought to the abbess in Barking, and she agreed to take him into the community. The nuns grew to love him dearly, especially a nun called Edith who taught him to read and write. Sadly the boy was struck by the plague; and with his dying breaths he called out: 'Edith! Edith! Edith!' As the boy's soul departed from his body, Edith was attacked by the same disease; and within a few days she followed him to God's heavenly kingdom. A few weeks later another of the nuns fell ill with the plague. As she lay dying in the middle of the night, she begged the sisters attending her to put out the lamp which burned by her bed. The sisters ignored her request. Then she said: ' You may think that my mind is wandering. But I can see such brightness in the room that the lamp appears to me as darkness.' She asked them again to put out the lamp, and again they ignored her. Finally she said: 'Let the lamp burn as long as you wish. I assure you that it gives me no light. My light comes from God; and it will reach its fullness when the light of dawn comes.'

6.7 The Deaths of Ethelburga and Tortgyth

Ethelburga, abbess of the monastery in Barking, survived the plague, and eventually died because her body had become utterly exhausted by hard work. The community also contained a nun from a noble family who for many years had been so crippled that she could hardly move her arms and legs. When she heard that her beloved abbess had departed this life, she asked to be carried into the chapel. For a day and a night she sat beside Ethelburga's body, which was awaiting burial. Then the crippled nun spoke to Ethelburga as if she were still alive; she begged the abbess to pray to God on her behalf, asking that God swiftly release her from the continual pain of her twisted limbs. Twelve days later she was set free from her body, exchanging her earthly troubles for a heavenly reward. Three years after Ethelburga's death another nun, called Tortgyth, contracted a wasting disease which over a period of months destroyed all her flesh; finally she could not even move her tongue. After three days and nights lying motionless on her bed, she suddenly looked upwards and spoke: 'I am so glad you have come; you are most welcome.' She remained silent for a few moments. Then she frowned and said: 'That is bad news. If it cannot be today, let it be soon.' After another interval of silence, she spoke a third time: 'That is better news. I shall be with you tomorrow night – it isn't long to wait.' The nuns attending her asked her to whom she had been speaking. 'To my dearest Ethelburga,' Tortgyth replied. The following night she died.

6.8 King Sebbi's Monastic Vocation

Sebbi, the king of the East Saxons, wanted God to be the true ruler of his kingdom. Thus on every decision he had to make, he always prayed for divine guidance. As the years passed, the burden of kingship became increasingly heavy on his shoulders; he yearned for the monastic life, abdicating his throne in favour of his son. He asked his wife if she would allow him to enter a monastery, but she adamantly refused, insisting that he should remain with her in the royal palace. Then, when he had been king for thirty years, he was attacked by a serious disease which confined him to his bed for most of the day. He asked his wife again for permission to enter a monastery; and on this occasion she reluctantly consented. Sebbi now went to Waldhere, who had succeeded Earconwald as bishop, to seek his permission also. Waldhere consented; and to Sebbi's great joy, he at last received the monastic robes. His illness continued to worsen, and the pain became almost intolerable. He became fearful that in his agony he might say something sinful, which would cause offence to others. So he asked Waldhere if only two people, whose discretion could be trusted, would attend him, and that no one else be allowed in his cell. In fact Sebbi uttered only words of praise and gratitude to God; and even as his body writhed with pain, his spirit remained serene.

Part 7

Hilda, Wilfred and Caedmon:
Conflicts and Visions at Whitby

7.1 Hilda's Convent at Hartlepool

Hilda was the niece of Edwin, the first king of Northumbria to allow the gospel to be preached there; and as a child she was baptised, along with her uncle, by Paulinus at York. The first half of her life, until the age of thirty-six, was spent in various secular occupations. Then she decided to devote herself wholly to God. Her elder sister was already a nun at Chelles in Gaul, so her initial intention was to spend the rest of her life in the same community, quietly devoting herself to prayer and study. But, after she had spent a year at Chelles, a message arrived from Aidan, begging her to return to Northumbria, and start a new convent on the north bank of the River Wear. This venture lasted only a few months, because she was unable to attract more than a handful of other women to join her. Aidan then asked her to be abbess of Hartlepool, a convent which he had founded some years earlier. Here Hilda enjoyed much greater success. During the first part of her life she had read deeply the Christian literature of both Britain and Europe, and had visited many wise Christian leaders. She now set about making Hartlepool a centre of Christian scholarship, as well as a place of fervent prayer. Soon Christians were coming from all over Britain and beyond the sea, to talk to Hilda, and to study the books which she had assembled.

7.2 Hilda's Community at Whitby

After Hilda had been abbess at Hartlepool for some years, she was asked to found a monastery at Whitby, where both men and women were to live in the same community. At Hartlepool, as in many religious communities of this time, the nuns had been allowed to retain some personal wealth and possessions; so there was a degree of material inequality between them. At Whitby everything was held in common, so that no one was rich or poor. She made Whitby an even brighter beacon of scholarship than Hartlepool, attracting kings and princes, as well as ordinary people, to come and study there. Soon Hilda herself became famous for the wisdom of her advice on every kind of matter. She constantly repeated that the source of all true wisdom is Scripture; and that those who want success in their vocation whatever it may be, should make a firm habit of reading and reflecting daily on a passage from the New Testament. Without doubt her most important work at Whitby was training young men to be priests and preachers, teaching them both to be skilled in expounding the gospel and to be fervent in applying the gospel to themselves. Five men from Whitby became bishops, including Wilfred – who later returned to Whitby for the famous Synod.

7.3 Conflict between British and Catholic Customs

While Hilda was creating at Whitby a beacon of spiritual light – indeed by happy coincidence the old British name for that place means 'Bay of the Beacon' – there was growing conflict concerning the two sets of Christian customs that flourished on this island. Those Christian bishops and priests who had trained in Kent and Gaul favoured the Catholic customs, introduced into Britain by Augustine. Those who had trained at such places as Iona and Lindisfarne followed the Irish customs, introduced into Britain by Columba. Aidan during his years at Lindisfarne became aware of this conflict, and was deeply troubled by it. While he himself remained loyal to Columba's teaching, he advocated mutual tolerance, saying that inner spiritual peace between Christians was far more important than the outward ways in which they express their faith. Sadly, however, Finan, Aidan's successor at Lindisfarne, was stubborn and intransigent, insisting that Columba's teaching should prevail throughout Britain. The main focus of controversy was the way in which the date of Easter was calculated. This led to particular confusion in the Northumbrian royal castle, where King Oswy celebrated Easter on the Irish date, while his wife Queen Eanfled, who was the daughter of the king of Kent, celebrated Easter on the Catholic date. So generally Oswy had finished Lent and was enjoying Easter, while Eanfled was still fasting.

7.4 The Convening of the Synod

When Finan died, he was replaced as abbot of Lindisfarne by Colman, who asserted the Irish customs even more strongly than Finan had. In the meantime Wilfred, a monk from Lindisfarne, had trained for the priesthood at Hilda's monastery in Whitby, and gone on to study theology in Gaul and Rome. On his return he instructed King Oswy's son, Alchfrid, in the Christian faith, teaching him that the Catholic ways are superior to the Irish ways. Alchfrid then gave Wilfrid a large expanse of land at Ripon on which to found a monastery. Under Wilfred's influence Alchfrid was now a staunch supporter of Catholic teaching, while his father continued to believe that Irish teaching was superior. Eventually the tension in the Northumbrian royal castle over this matter became unbearable, and Oswy decided that the dispute must be resolved. In the meantime bishops and priests from southern Britain were urging Wilfred and Alchfrid to assert the Catholic customs in Northumbria, in order to bring the entire British Church under the authority of Rome. Thus, in the year of our Lord 604, it was decided to hold a synod at Whitby, in which a final judgement could be made. Colman led those loyal to the Irish teaching supported by Cedd and Hilda herself; while Wilfred led those loyal to the Catholic teaching. Cedd, who spoke the languages of both the English and the British, acted as interpreter.

7.5 The Opening of the Synod

King Oswy presided at the great synod. When everyone had gathered, he gave a speech in which he described the synod's purpose: 'All of us worship a single God, and we all hope to go to the same heaven. They do not have different ways of worship in heaven, but everyone praises God in the same way at the same time. We must do the same on earth. Therefore we must decide which of the two traditions is correct; and when a decision has been made, all of us must loyally abide by it. I will ask the leaders of each group to speak in turn, explaining their customs.' Oswy asked Colman to begin. 'The Easter customs which I observe', Colman said, 'were taught to me by my superiors in Iona, who sent me to Lindisfarne. And all our forefathers, devout and holy men, observed these customs. Thus anyone who rejects them as wrong is also rejecting the men who practised them. Moreover, we believe that these customs originate with Saint John, the disciple especially loved by our Lord, and that he taught them to the churches he founded. So we maintain our customs in obedience to this great apostle and evangelist.'

7.6 Wilfred's Arguments

After Colman had finished, King Oswy commanded Wilfred to speak. 'The Easter customs which we observe', Wilfred began, 'are the same as those observed in Rome, where the blessed apostles Peter and Paul lived and where they died and are buried. Moreover, we have been told that these customs are also practised in Africa, Asia, Egypt and Greece – indeed in every nation and land where the Church of Christ has spread. The only people who are stupid enough to oppose these customs are these Scots, and their partners in obstinacy, the Picts and Britons, who inhabit only a portion of these remote islands on the edge of the world.' 'It is strange that you call us stupid,' Colman replied, 'when we uphold the customs taught by the apostle John. He was deemed worthy to lean on our Lord's breast, and his wisdom is respected throughout the world.' 'Far be it from us to call John himself stupid;' said Wilfred, 'he was continuing to observe the Law of Moses, because at that early time no Christian laws had been instituted in that place. But Peter, when he preached in Rome, abandoned the Jewish laws, and formulated customs that were specifically Christian. Thus we calculate the date of Easter according to Peter's teaching, which supercedes everything that went before.'

7.7 Colman's Defeat

'Are you asserting', Colman asked Wilfred, 'that our most revered father Columba, and all his successors, have been utterly misguided in their customs? Their holiness has been confirmed by numerous heavenly signs. And since I have no doubt that they are saints, I shall never cease to imitate their lives, customs and discipline.' 'There have been many others,' Wilfred replied, 'who have been equally holy and saintly, and yet have followed the correct rule about Easter. I do not deny that Columba and his successors were true servants of God. They loved God devoutly. But they were simple and primitive in their faith. I do not think that their Easter customs did them harm, because no one had shown them the correct customs. Indeed I feel sure that, if someone had taught them the Catholic customs, they would readily and joyfully have adopted them. After all, they obeyed all the laws of God which they had already learnt; so they surely would have obeyed the laws about

Easter, if these laws had been explained to them.' Colman did not answer these arguments.

7.8 Catholic Victory

'In conclusion,' Wilfred said, 'I wish to bring to mind the words of our Lord to the apostle who instituted our customs: Jesus called Peter the rock on which he would build his Church, and he gave Peter the keys to the age of heaven.' King Oswy turned to Colman: 'Is it true that our Lord spoke these words to Peter?' 'It is true, Your Majesty,' replied Colman. 'Can you show that similar authority was given to Columba?' asked the king. 'No,' answered Colman. 'If Peter has the key to heaven,' the king said to the whole assembly, 'I shall not contradict him. I shall obey his commands to the best of my knowledge and ability; otherwise when I arrive at the gates of heaven, he will not open them for me.' The majority of those present agreed with King Oswy's words, and indicated that in the future they would follow the Catholic customs. At this the king declared that the synod was over, and ordered everyone to disperse. Cedd, who had supported Colman, returned to the East Saxons, and ordered his priests to adopt the Catholic ways. But Colman and a few loyal followers remained obdurate.

7.9 Colman's Retreat

Colman and his disciples went northwards to the land of the Scots, to discuss with their compatriots their future course of action. King Oswy in the meantime installed a new bishop at Lindisfarne, called Tuda, who, like Oswy himself, had accepted the Catholic customs. Colman first went to Iona, where his opposition to the decision of the Whitby synod received a mixed reaction; some felt it right to submit to Catholic teaching, while others remained loyal to Columba's practices. Rather than allow this division to destroy the peace of the monastery, Colman took thirty of his most staunch supporters, and crossed the sea to Ireland. Initially Colman and his group went to a small island off the west coast, called Inishboffin – which means the Isle of the White Heifer. They were joined by a group of Irish monks, and together formed a monastery which observed the old customs in every detail. However, a dispute soon arose amongst them over food: the Irish monks liked to wander off in summer to visit friends, leaving Colman's group to gather the harvest; then as winter approached the Irish monks returned, expecting to share what the others had reaped. When the Irish monks refused to change their ways, Colman led his group to a new site on the mainland in Mayo. Their community now flourished, attracting numerous monks from Britain who still hankered for the ancient customs.

7.10 Hilda's Illness

Throughout her life Hilda had been aware of the differences between Catholic customs and the old British ways; and, although at Hartlepool and Whitby she had shown her respect for Columba and Aidan by following their example, she urged her monks and nuns to study Catholic teaching also. As a result she had no hesitation in accepting the decision of the synod. About ten years after the synod Hilda was struck down with a terrible illness which caused great pain within her stomach, and which also forced her frequently to retire to her cell with a high fever. She took this illness as a sign from God that she should devote herself more fully to prayer, leaving the administration of the monastery in the hands of others. Hilda now went frequently to stay at Hackness, a remote place in the hills behind Whitby, where she could live as a hermit. But she did not forget the spiritual care of her brothers and sisters. On the contrary whenever she was at Whitby she spent her time instructing them. She frequently gathered the entire community together, in order to expound the Scriptures to them; and she also invited individual monks and nuns to her cell for counsel.

Despite her physical suffering, she radiated great joy. As she herself frequently said: 'It is through suffering that we are made perfect; therefore we must give thanks to God, both in health and in sickness.'

7.11 *Caedmon's Dream*

Throughout the years that Hilda was abbess at Whitby, a man called Caedmon looked after the monastery's cattle. He was illiterate and also extremely shy. Every year a feast was held, to which all the workers, as well as the monks and nuns, were invited. After the meal a harp was handed round, and each person in turn was invited to sing. When Caedmon saw the harp approaching him, he would get up from the table and go back to the cattle-shed where he slept. In 680 Hilda presided at this feast for the last time; her illness finally killed her later that year. On this occasion when Caedmon returned to the cattle-shed, he had a strange dream. He saw a man standing beside him, who called him by name: 'Caedmon,' the man said, 'sing to me.' 'I don't know how to sing;' Caedmon replied, 'that is why I left the feast, and have come back here.' 'But you shall sing to me,' the man insisted. 'What shall I sing about?' Caedmon asked. 'Sing about the Creation,' the man replied. So Caedmon began to sing. And words poured from his lips in praise of God the Creator:

Praise the One who made the universe
Using the material of Heaven.
Glory be to his power and his wisdom.
He is the worker of all wonders.
He is the sustainer of the world.
He fashioned the human race,
Making Heaven their roof and Earth their mansion.

7.12 Caedmon's Song

No translation from Caedmon's language to our own can capture the beauty and dignity of the verses he sang. When he awoke, he remembered all that he had sung in the dream, and he added more verses in the same style.

In the morning he went to see the manager of the monastery lands, who was his superior, and told him about the gift he had received. The manager immediately took Caedmon to Hilda. Despite her great pain Hilda responded with enthusiasm to Caedmon's account of his dream; and she summoned the senior monks to hear his song, in order to assess its quality. Caedmon repeated the song to this august group, singing with a clear, pure voice which astonished them all. They agreed that Caedmon's gift had come from the Lord. To test him further they explained to him a passage of Scripture, and asked him to render it into verse; and the next morning he returned with another excellent poem, in which the spirit of the Scripture passage was expressed perfectly. Hilda was delighted that God had bestowed this gift on so humble a man. She urged him to give up his present occupation, and become a monk. And when he had entered the community, she arranged for her senior monks to teach him the entire story of God's love for the human race, as recorded in the Bible. He then re-told this story in a series of beautiful songs. And during the rest of his life he sang these songs to thousands of people, inspiring them to be more devout in their faith and generous in their actions.

Part 8

Theodore and Hadrian:
Laws and Doctrines at Hertford

8.1 *The Search for an Archbishop*

In the same year that the synod was held at Whitby, the sixth archbishop of Canterbury after Augustine, a man called Deusdedit, died. King Oswy of Northumbria and King Egbert of Kent met to discuss who should succeed Deusdedit; and they chose Wighard, a priest with long experience in Church administration. They sent Wighard to Rome, with letters to the Pope asking him to consecrate Wighard as archbishop; they also sent gifts of gold and silver Communion vessels. Wighard arrived in Rome, and explained his purpose to the Pope; but soon afterwards a plague swept the city, and Wighard died of it. The Pope took advice on whom he should consecrate as archbishop of the English, and was recommended an African called Hadrian, who was abbot of a monastery near Naples; Hadrian, like Wighard, was a skilled and experienced administrator. Hadrian refused, saying that he lacked the gifts needed for a good bishop; and he recommended Andrew, who was chaplain to a nearby convent. He too refused on the grounds of ill health. The Pope went back to Hadrian, pressing him to accept the office, but Hadrian asked for time to find a more suitable candidate.

8.2 Theodore's Appointment

Hadrian asked a monk in Rome called Theodore, a native of Tarsus from where the apostle Paul had come, if he would be archbishop of Canterbury. Theodore was already aged sixty-six; but Hadrian thought that his deep knowledge of both sacred and secular literature, combined with his reputation for honesty and fairness, made him a suitable candidate. Theodore agreed, on condition that Hadrian accompany him to Britain, since Hadrian was familiar with Gaul through which they would travel. Hadrian consented, and recommended Theodore to the Pope. The Pope for his part expressed concern that Theodore would try to introduce his Greek customs to the Church in Britain – which had only just accepted the Catholic customs of Rome. Hadrian undertook to prevent this. Theodore now allowed his hair to grow freely for four months, so that he could replace the Greek tonsure with the Roman one. Then in March 668, about four years after the death of the previous archbishop of Canterbury, the Pope consecrated Theodore to that office; and two months later he and Hadrian set off for Canterbury. Their journey took a further year, since Theodore's great age forced him to have frequent rests. Yet having arrived in Britain, Theodore's health proved remarkably robust, enabling him to serve the Church in Britain for over twenty-one years.

8.3 Assertion of Catholic Doctrine

Soon after his arrival, Theodore went on a tour, visiting every part of Britain, south of the Roman wall, which had submitted to Christ. Since he was the first archbishop of Canterbury to be appointed after the synod in Whitby, he wished to ensure that Catholic teaching was accepted throughout the Church in Britain; and as the primary representative of the Catholic Church he felt compelled to assert his own authority. Wherever he went he invited all the priests in the locality, and all those aspiring to the priesthood, to gather in one place. There he instructed them in the holy Scriptures, and taught them how to compose Christian songs. He also showed them how to calculate the dates of the Christian festivals, using the techniques of astronomy; and by this means he ensured that Easter was everywhere celebrated on the correct date. He encouraged those young priests with sufficient ability to learn Latin and Greek, thereby enabling them to drink from the great pool of Christian literature; and those priests who became fluent in these noble languages began to teach others, greatly enhancing the level of scholarship on this remote island. Knowing that his visits to each region were brief and infrequent, Theodore wished to ensure that there was a network of bishops of the highest calibre. Many places at this time had no bishop; others had bishops who were lazy or corrupt. Theodore dismissed the bad bishops. And in selecting men to fill the vacancies, he looked for three qualities: deep knowledge of the Scriptures; an ability to communicate that knowledge to the common people; and, above all, personal holiness.

8.4 The Council of Hertford

After deciding to adopt the Catholic teaching at the Synod of Whitby, King Oswy of Northumbria became fervent in his obedience to the Pope; and he hoped to travel to Rome in his old age, and to die there. But in 670, at the age of fifty-eight, he was struck down by a fatal illness; and his son Egfrid succeeded to the throne. Egfrid shared his father's devotion to Catholic customs and doctrine, and therefore supported Theodore in his campaign to assert the authority of the Catholic Church throughout Britain. Once his tour of Britain was complete Theodore decided to convene a council of bishops and senior priests, in order to pass laws by which the Church should be governed. The bishops and priests assembled in September 673 at Hertford. In his opening address Theodore declared himself unworthy to hold the high office of archbishop; but he urged the bishops and priests to accept his authority not on his own account, but in deference to the Pope in Rome, who is successor to the apostle Peter. He went on to say that the purpose of the laws they would pass was to promote peace and harmony within the Church; and therefore a spirit of peace and harmony should infuse their discussions. Theodore then held up a copy of the laws he had drafted in advance, saying that he had based each law firmly on the teachings of the early Fathers of the Christian Church. He asked the bishops in turn whether they wished to abide by these teachings. And each replied: 'Any rule or law laid down by the Fathers I will joyfully and willingly obey.'

8.5 Laws on Church Order

Theodore now read out to the bishops the laws which he proposed. The first four, which concerned authority within the Church, were as follows:

1. No bishop shall interfere in the diocese of another, but confine himself to the guidance of the people committed to his charge.

2. No bishop shall claim precedence over another bishop out of ambition; seniority of consecration alone shall determine precedence.

3. A priest shall not move from place to place, nor from church to church, without permission from his own bishop.

4. When travelling, bishops and priests shall be content with whatever hospitality is offered to them; and they shall not exercise any priestly functions without permission from the bishop in whose diocese they find themselves.

The other laws which Theodore proposed were:

5. All shall unite in observing the holy day of Easter on the Sunday after the fourteenth day of the moon of the first month.

6. More bishops shall be consecrated as the number of the faithful increases.

7. A synod shall be held of all the bishops in Britain twice a year.

8. No bishop shall interfere in any way with monasteries dedicated to God, nor take anything from them by force.

9. A monk shall not wander from place to place, nor from monastery to monastery, without written permission from his abbot.

8.6 Discussion and Decision

Seven of the nine laws on Church order which Theodore had drafted were passed by the bishops without argument. The proposal that the bishops should hold a synod twice a year provoked objections from bishops of the more remote dioceses, who drew attention to the length of their journeys. So Theodore agreed that a synod once a year would be adequate; it would be held in London at the beginning of August. The law proposing that more bishops be consecrated as the number of the faithful increases also raised anxieties, since it implied that the geographical size of dioceses would gradually decrease. They decided to delay any decision on this matter. Theodore also put forward a law concerning marriage: that no Christian man may leave his wife except on the grounds of fornication; and that, if he does so, he cannot take another wife – he must either remain single, or be reconciled to his wife. This was agreed. Theodore invited all the bishops to put their signatures to the laws they had passed. And it was unanimously decided that anyone who disobeyed the laws relating to Church order should be suspended from all priestly functions.

8.7 The Council of Hatfield

In the year of our Lord 680 Theodore learnt that the faith of the Church in Constantinople was being disturbed by the teaching of a man called Eutyches; and since in his youth he had known Constantinople well, Theodore was deeply upset. Eutyches maintained that Jesus Christ was purely divine, and hence his humanity was an illusion. To prevent this heresy from spreading to Britain, Theodore summoned the bishops plus a large number of priests to a second council, which took place on the Plain of Hatfield, near to Hertford. Theodore began by explaining to them the ideas which Eutycles was promulgating, and invited each in turn to respond. To his delight they all rejected these ideas, asserting that Jesus Christ was truly human, as well as truly divine. Theodore proclaimed that this was the true Catholic doctrine, as it had been formulated in the five General Councils of the Church. He recorded the loyalty of the English bishops to the Catholic faith in a special letter, which would guide all future generations on this island. Theodore also asked the bishops whether they regarded the Pope in Rome as their master and guide in matters of doctrine. The bishops were unanimous in their doctrinal submission to Rome, proclaiming that they wished neither to add to, nor subtract from, anything which the Pope taught. This too was recorded in the letter.

8.8 Reconciliation between Two Kings

During Theodore's period as archbishop, two Christian kings, Egfrid of Northumbria and Ethelred of Mercia, went to war against one another. They fought a fierce battle near the River Trent, at which Egfrid's brother, a young man aged only eighteen, was killed. This death made the hatred between the two kings even more bitter, and people feared that there would be a series of battles until one of the kings was killed. But Theodore went to visit each king in turn, urging them in Christ's name to set aside their anger, and offer the hand of friendship. He also persuaded Ethelred to offer gold in compensation for the death of Egfrid's brother. Thus peace was restored. Theodore was now a very old man, and was becoming increasingly frail. One night in a dream an angel spoke to him, telling him that he would die at the age of eighty-eight. Theodore related this dream to his friends, so preparation could be made for a successor. In September 690, when he had just reached eighty-eight, he fell ill and died. Yet despite the warning, it still took the kings and bishops two years to agree on a new archbishop. His name was Bertwald, the abbot of the monastery at Reculver, in Thanet; he was a skilled administrator, but manifestly lacked Theodore's vision.

Part 9

Chad and Coenred:
the Gospel in Mercia

9.1 *Peada's Conversion*

Penda, the king of Mercia, apparently had no religious feelings whatever. Thus when he invaded neighbouring kingdoms, such as Northumbria, and the land of the East Angles, he happily stole the precious objects from their churches. Yet equally he was indifferent to the religions which his own people followed; and this indifference allowed Christianity to begin spreading within Mercia even in Penda's life-time. Two men in particular pioneered the Christian mission to Mercia. The first was Cedd, a monk from Lindisfarne. As a young man on his own initiative he toured the remote regions of Mercia, telling people about Christ and winning converts. To his surprise Penda and his warriors never tried to hinder him. Cedd continued this work for several years until in 653 he was called to lead a mission to the East Saxons. But in that very year God provided a second pioneer, in the person of Penda's own son, called Peada. This noble and gentle young man went to visit Oswy, king of the Northumbrians, and asked for his daughter's hand in marriage. Oswy agreed on condition that Peada became a Christian. So the monks of Lindisfarne instructed Peada in the faith; and Peada was impressed with all he learnt. At the end of the instruction he declared that he would gladly become a Christian, even if marriage to the princess were refused. Finan, the abbot of Lindisfarne, baptised Peada at the village of Walton, where the

East Saxon king, Sigbert, was also baptised. Oswy then consented to the marriage; and Peada returned to Mercia with his new wife, determined to teach others the faith he had acquired.

9.2 Oswy's Victory over Penda

Despite the marriage of his son to Oswy's daughter, Penda continued to attack Northumbria in order to steal its wealth. Oswy grew so weary of these attacks that he offered Penda a vast quantity of gold and jewels on condition that he left Northumbria in peace. Penda refused, declaring that he intended to wipe out the entire Northumbrian nation, from the highest noble to the humblest peasant. Oswy prayed to God for strength to defend his kingdom, promising that if he were to defeat Penda, he would build twelve monasteries and convents, and he would offer his youngest daughter as a nun to one of them. He then gathered his troops and marched southwards. But when Oswy saw Penda's warriors, he realised that they outnumbered his own army by more than thirty to one. Despite these terrible odds, Oswy decided to attack at once; and his men fought with such courage and skill that they defeated the Mercians, killing Penda himself and all his commanders. Oswy kept his promise, building six monasteries in Deira and six in Bernicia. He gave his daughter, who was only one year old, to the convent at Hartlepool, which at that time was ruled by Hilda – who later became the famous abbess at Whitby. Oswy appointed Peada to rule the southern part of Mercia.

9.3 Wulfere's Accession and Chad's Appointment

Oswy's victory over Mercia lasted only three years. At Easter, six months after Penda's defeat, Peada was murdered – probably by his own wife, who was Oswy's eldest daughter. This evil woman then encouraged Peada's younger brother, called

Wulfhere, to rebel against Oswy. Wulfhere at this time was not yet an adult; yet he gradually gathered support from the Mercian chieftains, and then declared himself king. He and his followers drove out all the officials whom Oswy had appointed to govern Mercia, and again took control of their own land. But although in killing Peada he had extinguished one of the spiritual beacons of Mercia, Wulfhere acknowledged Christ as the true light. During the seventeen years of his rule Wulfhere appointed a succession of very able and holy men as bishops of Mercia. The third and most remarkable of these was called Chad. As a young man Chad had gone to live as a monk in Ireland. He then returned to Britain to become a disciple of Aidan in Lindisfarne. While he was there Etheldreda came to Northumbria to marry the king; and she chose Chad as her chaplain. After Etheldreda left Northumbria, Chad became abbot at Lastingham, the monastery founded by his brother Cedd. He was then persuaded to leave the monastic life again, to become Bishop of York; and it was from York that he moved to Mercia.

9.4 Chad's Way of Life

Chad had been appointed Bishop of York by Oswy, King of Northumbria. But when Theodore became Archbishop of Canterbury, he declared that Chad's consecration as bishop was invalid, because the other bishops who had performed the rite were supporters of the old British customs, rather than the Catholic customs. Chad accepted this judgement without protest, saying to Theodore: 'I willingly resign my office, since I have never deemed myself worthy of it.' On learning of Chad's resignation, Wulfhere immediately invited him to Mercia. Initially Chad was reluctant to go, preferring to return to the peaceful life of Lastingham. But Wulfhere persuaded both Chad to accept, and Theodore to agree to his appointment. Chad rode to his home in the town of Lichfield, building a house near the church for himself and seven or eight brethren whom he had brought from Lastingham. They met daily for worship and study; and when Chad himself was touring Mercia to preach the gospel, the brethren praying constantly for the Holy Spirit to inspire him. At first Chad followed Aidan's example of travelling only on foot, so that he could talk to the ordinary people he met on the lanes and paths. But Theodore, the archbishop of Canterbury, was insistent that all bishops should assert the dignity of their office by travelling on horseback. Chad had never mounted a horse before, and so was compelled to take lessons; thereafter he obediently followed Theodore's instructions. Despite this unwanted privilege, the people of Mercia quickly recognised Chad as a bishop of outstanding sanctity.

9.5 Chad's Teaching

Chad became renowned amongst the Mercian people for the awe and respect in which he held the forces of nature, believing that all natural events contain messages from God. Whenever a violent storm arose, with thunder and lightning, he rushed into the nearest church, and lay prostrate before the altar. When people asked him why he did this, he replied: 'God stirs the air, makes the lightning flash and prompts thunder to roll. He does these things to make people fear him, reminding them of his final judgement. Thus he shatters their pride and drowns their arrogance, bringing to their minds an image of the Last Day when the earth itself will burst into flames, and the heavens will fill with clouds of pitch black. So when a storm rises, we fall to the ground in prayer, begging forgiveness of our sins, and imploring God in his mercy to cleanse our inmost hearts – and thus make us fit for heaven.'

9.6 Chad's Death

Chad had been bishop in Mercia for only two and a half years when a terrible plague struck. Lichfield was hit with particular severity, and most of Chad's congregation died. Then Chad himself, who had comforted the sick night and day, finally succumbed. He was compelled to retire to his room and await death. One of his brothers was passing the door of his room when he heard a voice singing; the sound had such purity that he presumed an angel was visiting his beloved bishop. He entered the room and found Chad alone. Chad asked him to summon to the room the other brethren. When the brethren had assembled. Chad gave them his last instructions: 'Live in love and peace with one another. Stick closely to the monastic rules which I have taught you. And be always willing to listen to the insights of others; even the humblest follower of Christ can sometimes speak wisely.' He then lay back in his bed and sighed. After a long pause he spoke again: 'The welcome guest who has already visited many in our congregation is about to visit me. Please go to the church, and pray for the salvation of my soul.' The brethren did as their bishop asked; and while they were in the church, Chad quietly died.

9.7 Ethelred's Attack on Kent

When Chad died, Wulfhere was still king of the Mercian people. Soon afterwards Wulfhere himself died, and was succeeded by his brother Ethelred. Like Wulfhere, Ethelred combined genuine devotion to Christ with a capacity for terrible cruelty. In the year 676 he made war on Kent, looting and destroying numerous churches and monasteries without inhibition or guilt. The climax of this barbaric frenzy was at Rochester, where he and his soldiers laid waste to the entire town, including its cathedral. The bishop of Rochester at the time was a humble, unworldly man called Putta, who was driven at the point of the sword from his altar. In a strange and unexpected way, reparation was eventually made for the expulsion of Putta. A few months before Ethelred's attack on Kent, Theodore had appointed Sexwulf as Bishop of Mercia. When Sexwulf heard about the destruction of Rochester, he invited Putta to come and live in Mercia, where he gave him a small church and a house. Putta accepted Sexwulf's offer, and spent the rest of his days there. Thus Putta's presence in Mercia was a constant reminder to Ethelred of his wicked cruelty. In the meantime Theodore appointed a new bishop for Rochester, called Cuichelm; but when he saw the ruins of the cathedral, Cuichelm felt unequal to the task of rebuilding it, and immediately resigned. So Theodore appointed Gebmund in his place, a tough and able administrator who set about the task of reconstruction with energy and determination.

9.8 Coenred's Christian Rule

Ethelred was succeeded to the throne of Mercia by his nephew Coenred, who radiated the love of Christ to all whom he encountered. As king he believed his primary concern should be the spiritual well-being of his subjects; and to this end he frequently visited people in their homes, especially those who were sick, to bring comfort and encouragement. He also convened meetings in towns and villages, where he would speak to the inhabitants about Christian morality. Coenred also set about reforming the behaviour of the Mercian army, which was notorious throughout Britain for its savagery. Coenred was tireless in talking to officers and soldiers alike about the importance of restraint, as well as courage, in times of war – and of honesty and fidelity in their private lives. Coenred's efforts met with considerable success. But there was one particular officer, in a very senior position in the Mercian army, who was utterly impervious to Coenred's teaching. Coenred frequently summoned this man to talk about the gospel; but, while the officer professed the Christian faith, he refused to apply his faith either to his work or to his personal affairs, saying that he would make amends at some future date. This caused Coenred great grief and frustration.

9.9 Coenred's Ministry to a Dying Soldier

One day the senior officer, whom King Coenred had been urging to repent, fell ill, and was forced to take to his bed. The pains soon became so severe that his life was clearly in danger. Coenred went to see him, begging him to repent of his sins before he died. But the officer again refused, saying that he did not want his friends to accuse him of repenting out of fear of death. As he spoke, his lips curled into a smile, since he believed his words were brave – so others would admire him when they heard he had not repented. The illness continued to worsen. Eventually the king went to the dying soldier again. The man was now utterly miserable, and cried out: 'What do you want now? Why have you come to see me? It's too late to help or save me.' 'Stop talking like a madman,' the king replied. 'I'm not mad,' the man said; 'I have had a vision in which all my wickedness has been set before me. The book recording my good deeds was shown to me, and it was a single page; then the book recording my bad deeds was shown, and it was huge. I know now that I am damned to burn for ever.' Coenred assured him that even at this late stage forgiveness was possible, if he only would repent. But the man was so convinced of his own damnation that for the remaining hours of his life he simply sobbed in self-pity. Coenred ensured that the story of this man's death was spread throughout his kingdom, to encourage others to repent while they had time.

9.10 Coenred's Retirement to Rome

Coenred ruled Mercia for many years, bringing peace and prosperity to its people. Unlike his predecessors who often made war on neighbouring kingdoms, Coenred offered the hand of friendship. As a result the young men of Mercia could remain on their lands, rather than enlist as soldiers. At last Coenred decided that he should turn his attention away from earthly matters towards heavenly matters. He passed his crown and sceptre to his cousin Coelred and set off for Rome. There he entered a monastery and took vows as a monk; and he devoted the rest of his days to prayer and to acts of charity. News of Coenred's departure for Rome soon spread across Britain. Offa, a gentle and handsome young man who had recently become king of the East Saxons, was especially impressed, and felt called to follow Coenred. He asked his wife for permission to leave her. He then gave up his crown and sceptre, and began the long journey to Rome. On arrival he went to the monastery where Coenred was living, and asked if he too could be received as a monk. And like Coenred he devoted the rest of his life to prayer and acts of charity.

Part 10

Wilfred:
the Abbot of Ripon

10.1 *Wilfred's Youth*

As a boy Wilfred was studious and thoughtful. He was always polite to adults, showing special respect for priests and monks; and people frequently remarked at his maturity. His mother died when he was young; but Wilfred was so well behaved that his father had little trouble in bringing him up alone. At the age of fourteen Wilfred decided to become a monk, and his father readily agreed to this praiseworthy aspiration. So he went to Lindisfarne, where he offered himself as a servant to the brethren. He worked hard at the community's manual work, and endeared himself to the monks by his promptness and eagerness in obeying their orders. Having a quick mind he soon learnt the psalms and prayers which the monks recited; and at an exceptionally young age he was allowed to take vows, to become a full member of the monastery. But after a few years at Lindisfarne Wilfred had become impatient with the narrow attitudes and primitive customs of his brethren; and wanted to go abroad to widen his knowledge. So he went to Eanfled, the queen of Northumbria, to ask for her support. She was cousin to the king of Kent, and longed for the more sophisticated Catholic customs which the churches in Kent had always practised. She recognised Wilfred's intellectual gifts, and saw him as the means by which Catholic customs could be brought to Northumbria. So she advised Wilfred to travel to Rome, and gave him material help for his journey, urging him to return home as soon as he had learnt the Catholic doctrines and styles of worship.

10.2 *Visit to Rome*

Wilfred first went to Kent, with a letter from Eanfled recommending him to her cousin, the king. While he was there, Wilfred observed carefully all the religious practices, which followed the Catholic teachings. He met another man, called Biscop, who was later to become abbot of Wearmouth, and they decided to travel to Rome together. When they arrived at Lyons in southern Gaul the elderly bishop of the city was deeply impressed by Wilfred's wise conversation, graceful manners, and his enthusiasm for improving the Christian Church, as well as his mature and balanced opinions. So the bishop invited Wilfred to remain in Lyons, and take over the administration of a large area of his diocese. Wilfred replied that he must first study in Rome, but agreed to stay in Lyons for a longer period on his return. As soon as he reached Rome, Wilfred set himself the task of observing every aspect of Church life there – its worship, its administration, its law and its finances. He won the friendship of a senior cleric called Boniface, who was one of the Pope's advisors; and Boniface revealed to him the inner workings of the papal offices. Eventually Wilfred felt he understood the Church in Rome perfectly, and went back to Lyons. He remained there for three years, taking over an increasing proportion of the bishop's activities. The bishop was about to name Wilfred as his successor when the old man was murdered.

10.3 *Appointment as Abbot*

On his return to Britain Wilfred went to visit Alchfrid, the eldest son of Oswy, king of Northumbria. Oswy had made

Alchfrid the governor of Deira, the southern part of his kingdom around the city of York. There was now growing rivalry
between father and son, especially over religious matters, since
Oswy still practised the old customs introduced by Columba
and Aidan, while Alchfrid favoured the Catholic customs.
Alchfrid saw Wilfred as a valuable ally in this conflict, and with
Wilfred's support began to assert his Catholic convictions. At
Ripon there was a large monastery which adhered to the old
customs. Alchfrid ordered the monks to adopt Catholic practices; the monks refused, and Alchfrid expelled them. Alchfrid
then appointed Wilfred as abbot; and Wilfred recruited monks
who were willing to obey the Catholic rules. Alchfrid now decided that, although Wilfred was only thirty years of age, he
should become Bishop of York. During his journey to Rome
Wilfred had met the bishop of Paris, who had been impressed
with Wilfred's character and intellectual abilities. So Alchfrid
sent Wilfred to Paris, with a letter requesting the bishop to consecrate Wilfred. Before leaving for Paris, Wilfred went to
Whitby, to attend the synod called by King Oswy. Wilfred led
the group advocating Catholic doctrines and customs; and to
Alchfrid's delight, Wilfred's views prevailed.

10.4 *Appointment to and Expulsion from York*

When Wilfred arrived in Paris, the bishop of that city recognised Wilfred as a man of growing influence and importance.
He gathered eleven other bishops from nearby dioceses, and together they consecrated Wilfred as bishop. In the meantime
King Oswy, against the wishes of his son Alchfrid, appointed
Chad as Bishop of York. Thus when Wilfred returned to Britain
he was barred from entering the city, and was forced to retire to
his monastery at Ripon. Chad remained in York for three years,
governing the Church in that diocese with great wisdom.
Finally Theodore, the new archbishop of Canterbury, intervened
in the dispute sending Chad to Mercia, and appointing Wilfred

to York. But soon afterwards, in the year of our Lord 670, King Oswy was struck down by a fatal illness; and as he lay dying, he nominated Egfrid, his second son, as his successor. Eight years later Egfrid felt sufficiently confident of his own authority to expel Wilfred from York; and in his place he appointed two bishops, one living in York itself, and the second living at Hexham. Wilfred decided to go to Rome to plead his case before the Pope, and set sail for Gaul. To his dismay a strong westerly wind drove his ship to Frisia, the flat Germanic land at the mouth of the Rhine. It was now late autumn, and he felt compelled to spend the winter there. He spent his time preaching the gospel to the Frisian people; and although many thousands heard his words of truth, few were converted.

10.5 Mission to the South Saxons

In the spring Wilfred continued his journey to Rome. And there he laid charges against Egfrid for expelling him from his diocese; and he argued that the appointment of two new bishops in his place was invalid. The Pope and several other bishops heard his case, and concluded that his case was just, declaring that he should be restored to the diocese of York. Wilfred now returned to Britain; but, despite the Pope's support, Egfrid remained hostile. So Wilfred made his way to the province of the South Saxons, which lies to the west of Kent along the southern coast of Britain. The king of the South Saxons, called Ethelwalh, had recently become a Christian under the influence of King Wulfhere of Mercia; and when Ethelwalh was baptised, Wulfhere became his godfather. Thus Ethelwalh invited Wilfred to instruct his nobles and officers in the Christian faith, and to baptise them. Wilfred also taught the South Saxon people how to fish. Although the rivers of their province were rich in all kinds of fish and eels, the South Saxons had no means of catching them. So Wilfred showed them how to make nets. As a result the people never again went hungry. Wilfred himself did not penetrate the remoter regions of the province. But as the production of fishing-nets spread, so his name became famous. This meant that in subsequent years, when Christian monks travelled to every village and farm, the people were open to their message. One of these monks, called Dicul, established a monastery at Chichester, which became the spiritual centre of the South Saxon province.

10.6 *Appointment to Hexham*

While Wilfred was living amongst the South Saxons, Theodore, the archbishop of Canterbury, was seeking to restore Wilfred to the bishopric of York. Egfrid, the king of Northumbria, was impervious to Theodore's entreaties. But four years after Wilfred's return from Rome, Egfrid died; and the new king, Aldfrid, was willing to negotiate with Theodore. In the year of our Lord 687 Aldfrid agreed that Wilfred could come back to York with a much smaller area under his charge: he would be bishop of the city of York and the surrounding countryside, and could again be abbot of Ripon. Wilfred agreed to this compromise. But relations between Aldfrid and Wilfred soon deteriorated; and five years later Wilfred was expelled from York for a second time. Wilfred now travelled southwards to Mercia, where King Ethelred, and later King Coenred, eagerly supported the Catholic doctrines and customs. Wilfred founded a number of monasteries there, including one at Oundle and another at Peterborough. Then in 703 he went again to Rome to plead his case; and again the Pope judged in his favour, condemning Aldfrid's actions – just as Egfrid's actions had earlier been condemned. By the time Wilfred came back to Britain, Aldfrid had died and a teenage boy called Osred had succeeded to the throne of Northumbria. Wilfred and Osred met on the banks of the River Nidd; and Osred agreed that Wilfred could be bishop in Hexham, and be restored as abbot of Ripon. For the last four years of his tumultuous life Wilfred lived in peace. He died in 709 while visiting his monastery in Oundle; and the monks carried his body back to his first monastery in Ripon, where he was buried on the south side of the altar.

Part 11

Cuthbert:
the Hermit of Farne Island

11.1 Cuthbert's Childhood

For the first years of his life, Cuthbert was interested only in playing with other children. He loved every kind of game and prank; and since he was naturally agile and quick-witted, he won most games he played. He would be fresh when the other children were exhausted; and he would look round in triumph, teasing them for their feebleness. He used to boast that he had beaten all the children of his own age, and many who were older, at wrestling, jumping and running. One day Cuthbert was playing with friends in a field, rushing about in great excitement, when a child aged only three ran up to him. With the gravity of an old man, the child rebuked Cuthbert for his idleness and self-indulgence, saying that he should learn to control himself. When Cuthbert guffawed with laughter, the child threw himself to the ground and burst into tears. The other children tried to comfort him, but to no avail. Then Cuthbert himself pleaded with the child to stop crying. But the child rebuked Cuthbert again: 'Why do you persist in your silly behaviour, letting the gifts which God has bestowed on you go to waste?' The words pierced Cuthbert's heart. He hugged the child, thanking him for his wisdom, and then returned home. He never again played with his friends, and his demeanour became earnest and solemn.

11.2 *Vision in the Sky*

Cuthbert became a shepherd, looking after a flock which belonged to a neighbouring family. This required him to spend many nights up in the hills where the sheep grazed. There he would meet other shepherds, and they would stay together for companionship and mutual protection. Usually, as the night wore on, the other shepherds would fall asleep, while Cuthbert kept himself awake praying. One night, when he was aged about seventeen, the skies suddenly lit up, and he could hear singing. Then he saw a ball of light rising from the earth, and disappearing into the cloud. At first he could not understand this vision. But he knew that it was a glimpse of heaven; and at that moment he dedicated himself to doing whatever was necessary to attain the eternal joys of heaven. The other shepherds slept through these events. When they awoke at dawn Cuthbert related the vision to them; and one of the shepherds suggested that the ball of light could have been a very holy soul being taken up to heaven. Later that day he led the sheep back to his home; and when he arrived, he was told that Aidan, the abbot of Lindisfarne, had died the previous night. At once Cuthbert delivered the sheep back to their owner, and began preparing himself to enter a monastery.

11.3 *Arrival at Melrose*

Cuthbert was aware of the high reputation which the monastery at Lindisfarne enjoyed. But Boisil, the prior at Melrose, was especially famous for his virtue and wisdom; so he decided to offer himself there as a monk. He travelled to Melrose carrying a sword and spear for protection. When he arrived, Boisil happened to be standing at the monastery gates. Cuthbert laid down the sword and spear at Boisil's feet; then Boisil directed Cuthbert to the church, where the young man prayed for God's blessing. When Cuthbert emerged from the church, Cuthbert told Boisil of his desire to become a monk. Boisil could see at once Cuthbert's potential for holiness, and welcomed him warmly. Cuthbert was told the rule of the monastery, and from the day of his arrival onwards he observed it in every detail. Indeed he exceeded the other monks in his zeal, praying, studying and working harder than anyone else. Although the monastic rule did not require this, he abstained from all alcoholic drink. But with regard to food he was more generous with himself, in order that his work would not suffer. He had retained the physical strength and agility which he enjoyed as a child, and he wished to put this gift to the service of the community.

11.4 Plague at Melrose

One year a plague swept across northern Britain, and Cuthbert was struck down by it. The other monks were appalled, because they had come to depend on his wisdom and holiness. They spent the entire night praying for his recovery. They did not tell Cuthbert in advance of their vigil, but the following morning one of the monks mentioned it to him. 'Then I should not be lying here,' Cuthbert replied; 'God will certainly have heard the prayers of so many good men. Please fetch me my shoes and stick.' So Cuthbert rose out of bed and began to move about with a stick. Day by day his strength returned; soon he was fully healed, apart from a pain in his thigh – which remained with him for the rest of his life. But now Boisil, who was an old man, began to weaken. 'Death is coming upon me,' he said; 'in a week's time my body and voice will have lost their strength.' 'Then I must use these seven days to learn from you,' answered Cuthbert. So throughout the next seven days, Boisil and Cuthbert studied the Gospel of St John, with Boisil explaining the true meaning of each passage. And at the end of the seventh day, when they had finished the final chapter, Boisil quietly died.

11.5 Mission to the Hill People

On Boisil's death Cuthbert became prior at Melrose; he was only twenty-seven years of age. He ruled the monks not by orders but by example and by the wisdom of his spiritual counsel. Indeed he devoted much of his time to private conversation; helping each monk in turn to discern God's will and purpose. He also frequently went out of the monastery to preach the gospel in the surrounding farms and villages, urging people to give up their foolish ways, and to strive instead for the joys of heaven. He was especially concerned for those who had earlier received the faith, but had reverted to their heathen ways. Some Christians, when they fell sick, even put their faith in incantations and magical amulets, instead of enthusing themselves to God, their creator. Sometimes Cuthbert travelled on horseback, but more often he went on foot from place to place. When he arrived at a village the people usually gathered round him, to hear his words. His exceptional eloquence was matched by the radiance of his spirit, so that many who heard him freely confessed their sins to him, begging forgiveness. Cuthbert made a particular effort to visit the remotest places, high up in the mountains, which were so poor and cold that other preachers rarely came. Often he was away from his monastery for a whole week, or even a fortnight, sharing the conditions of these rough mountain dwellers, and directing their eyes towards heaven.

11.6 Night Prayer

When he was at home in the monastery, Cuthbert rose from his bed each night, and went out to pray; he returned just in time for morning prayers. Usually none of the monks saw him, because they were asleep. But one night one of the monks was lying awake, and noticed Cuthbert creeping out of the dormitory. This monk decided to get up and follow him. Cuthbert went down to the river and waded out into the water until his entire body up to his shoulders was submerged. He remained there, praying and singing psalms, until the first light of dawn. Then he came out and knelt down on the bank. Two otters also came out, and lay down beside him, warming his feet with their breath, and trying to dry his body with their fur. When the sun had risen, Cuthbert blessed the otters, and they slipped back into the water. He walked home, and joined the other monks in church. Later that day the monk who had watched Cuthbert was so overwhelmed with guilt that he threw himself at Cuthbert's feet and confessed what he had done. 'I will forgive you,' said Cuthbert, 'but you must promise not to tell anyone, while I am still alive, of what you have seen.'

11.7 Reform at Lindisfarne

The monasteries at Lindisfarne and Melrose had the same abbot, who was also the bishop of the Northumbrian people. At this time the post was filled by a man called Eata. After Cuthbert had served for many years as prior of Melrose, Eata transferred him to Lindisfarne, to be prior there. The monks at Lindisfarne had become lax and self-indulgent, and Eata wanted Cuthbert to restore discipline. He showed great patience, hoping that his good example would gradually alter their attitudes. At the regular meetings, when the monks gathered to discuss matters of common concern, bitter insults were hurled at Cuthbert. But he never allowed himself to become angry, remaining calm and unruffled; and the next day he would be warm and pleasant towards his persecutors, as if nothing had happened. Moreover, although he often felt profoundly sad at the monks' stubbornness, he always wore a cheerful face. In this way he gradually won their respect. At Lindisfarne Cuthbert became even more zealous than at Melrose at keeping vigil, and often stayed awake in prayer for three or four nights at a stretch. During the day he drove away the urge to sleep by undertaking vigorous manual work, or by visiting the sick and the elderly on the island. He also frequently left Lindisfarne to preach the gospel in the surrounding villages, walking from village to village, farm to farm, as he had done near Melrose.

11.8 Retreat to Farne

For many years Cuthbert had yearned to live as a hermit, and he had prayed that one day God would make this possible. He believed that monk should spend the first part of his life in the active service of his brethren and the common people; and he regarded solitude as the reward for such service. Thus when he reached the age of forty he went to live in a more secluded place within Lindisfarne, in order to prepare himself both spiritually and physically. He spent many hours each day in solitary prayer, and ate only the most meagre portions of food. After two years of practising to be a hermit, Cuthbert sailed to Farne Island. This lies a few miles to the south-east of Lindisfarne, and to its east lies the limitless ocean. There he built a small oratory for prayer, and a hut in which to live. Both buildings were circular, constructed from rough stones and peat which he found on the island itself; their roofs were made from rough-hewn timbers and straw. Near the landing-place he made a larger house for guests. There was no fresh water on the island, so a group of young monks came from Lindisfarne to dig a well.

11.9 The Birds and the Seed

At first monks from Lindisfarne brought bread for Cuthbert to eat. But he decided that he should live by his own labour. So he asked them to bring seeds and a spade with which to dig the land. In the spring he sowed the seeds, which were wheat; but by mid-summer none had grown. 'It's either the nature of the ground,' he said to his brethren, 'or the will of God. I will try barley instead. If that fails, I will return to the monastery. It would be better to eat by my own labour there, than stay here depending on the labour of others.' So, although it was late in the year, the monks brought him barley seeds, which he planted immediately. And these quickly sprang up, bearing a good crop. However, as soon as the barley began to ripen, birds flew down and set about devouring it. Cuthbert came out and spoke to the birds: 'Why are you eating crops which you did not sow? Perhaps you have greater need for them than I have. If God has given you permission, then do as he bids. If not, stop stealing my food and go away.' The birds seemed to understand Cuthbert's words, and flew away. Never again did they eat crops which Cuthbert had sown.

11.10 Ravens and the Guest-House Roof

Ravens had long inhabited the island which Cuthbert now made his home. One day Cuthbert saw them tearing the straw from the guest house, and taking it away to build their nests. Cuthbert rebuked them; and with a wave of his right hand told them to leave his property alone. The ravens ignored him, and continued tearing the straw. 'How dare you defy me!' Cuthbert shouted; and he ordered them to leave at once. They were frightened he would attack them, so they flew away. Afterwards the ravens felt guilty at what they had been doing. And three days later one of them returned. Cuthbert was digging, and the bird flew down to his feet and stood before him; it spread out its wings and bowed its head. Cuthbert realised that it was apologising and begging his forgiveness. Cuthbert was overjoyed at the raven's repentance and invited all the ravens to return. They came back, carrying in their beaks a lump of pig's lard, to offer as a gift. Cuthbert put the lard in the guest house. The ravens stayed on the island, building their nests with grass and twigs which they found for themselves. Cuthbert invited guests to grease their shoes with the lard, telling them how he had obtained it. 'None of us is too virtuous to learn lessons from the birds,' he would add.

11.11 Visitors to Farne

Once the brethren from Lindisfarne had helped Cuthbert to build his hermitage, he lived completely alone. But countless visitors rowed across the choppy waters from the mainland to see Cuthbert and to ask his advice on spiritual matters. When he saw a boat arrive, Cuthbert went down to the landing-stage to welcome the visitors. He took them into the guest house and washed their feet in warm water. Then he led them one by one to the oratory, where they could each speak to him in private. They confessed their sins to him, and confided in him the temptations they faced, asking for his guidance on how to overcome them. No one left Farne Island disappointed; all were able to lay at Cuthbert's feet the spiritual and moral burdens with which they had arrived, and to return light of heart. Those who were beset with worry and anxiety, he filled with peace and tranquillity. He showed to everyone that good fortune and bad fortune alike are transitory, and that true and permanent happiness can only be found through faith in God. He also taught that the devil does not only catch wicked men and women in his net; all those who are merely luke-warm in their love are susceptible to the devil's tricks.

11.12 Teaching on Monastic Life

Those who came to visit Cuthbert at Farne Island often envied the apparent serenity of his way of life. 'Far from being serene,' replied Cuthbert, 'the life of a hermit involves constant battle. Devils come to me night and day, filling my breast with every kind of temptation. They want to smash my soul onto the rocks. And the worst and most dangerous temptations are those which

appear virtuous. Many times I have wondered whether to retreat from the battle-field; but as yet the devils haven't
wounded me, either in soul or in body.' As Cuthbert spoke in
these terms, the visitors' envy would turn to admiration. But
Cuthbert urged his visitors not to marvel at his way of life. 'It is
not especially praise-worthy', he said, 'to cast aside the cares of
the world and live alone. The people you should admire most
are the monks who remain within their community. They have
the hardest challenge of all: to obey their abbot. The decisions
of the abbot determine their times of prayer, their periods of
fasting, and the manual work they do. And the monks must
learn to submit to the abbot's will without complaint.'

11.13 Acceptance of the Bishopric

When Cuthbert had been a young man at Melrose, Boisil, the
old prior, had prophesied that Cuthbert would eventually become a bishop. Cuthbert had always trembled at this prospect;
but he knew in his heart that Boisil's prophecy came from God.
While he was living on Farne Island, so many visitors came to
visit him that his reputation for holiness and wisdom spread far
and wide. Thus when the Church in Northumbria needed a new
bishop, the people demanded that Cuthbert be chosen; and a
synod of all the clergy was held at which they too decided that
Cuthbert be appointed bishop. A letter was sent to him, requesting him to become bishop. But at first Cuthbert refused.
Then a group of clergy sailed across to Farne Island, begging
him to accept. Still he refused. Finally the king himself, accompanied by numerous nobles and ordinary peasants, went to
Farne Island in a fleet of ships. Cuthbert saw the ships arriving,
and remained in his hut, hoping they would go away. The king
and his nobles called out, pleading with him to see them. After
some minutes he emerged, and the king and the nobles knelt at
his feet, with tears pouring down their cheeks. 'For the salvation of our souls,' the king said, 'we ask you to be our

bishop.' Very reluctantly Cuthbert submitted to their pleas, and accepted the yoke of episcopacy.

11.14 Episcopal Ministry

Cuthbert became bishop of the Northumbrian people in 685 after he had lived on Farne Island for nine years. He accepted the office in late autumn; but, since so many wished to attend the service of consecration, it was delayed until the weather improved in the following spring. During this time he continued to live at his hermitage, preparing himself by prayer and fasting. As soon as he had been consecrated he began to travel around Northumbria, visiting his flock. In every village he asked to be taken to those who were sick or in any kind of mental distress. Through his words, and through leading them in prayer, he brought comfort and encouragement; and frequently in the hours and days following his visit they recovered. He also asked to meet those who were notorious for their evil ways, and urged them to repent. Although as bishop he could have enjoyed many material comforts and luxuries, Cuthbert maintained the strict frugality he had observed since his youth, and he adhered to the monastic routine in whatever circumstances he found himself. Any money or gifts that well-wishers offered him were either refused or immediately handed on to the poor and destitute.

11.15 Visit to Herbert

A hermit called Herbert lived on an island in the middle of the lake from which the River Derwent flows. Once a year Herbert used to leave his island and go to Cuthbert, in order to receive Cuthbert's counsel and guidance on spiritual matters. Before he went to Cuthbert Herbert usually felt spiritually cold, his passion for Christ burnt out by the exertion of continual prayer.

But after a few days with Cuthbert the fire of divine love was rekindled. When Herbert came to see Cuthbert in the year 686, Cuthbert's counsel was especially profound. Then, shortly before Herbert was due to leave, Cuthbert said casually: 'Dear brother, ask me now your final questions. This is the last time we shall see each other with eyes of flesh. By next year I shall have laid aside this earthly tabernacle, and departed.' Herbert flung himself at Cuthbert's feet and sobbed. 'In God's name do not leave me,' he cried; 'pray to God that, just as we have served him together on earth, so we may travel together to see his glory in heaven.' Cuthbert knelt down on the ground to pray, remaining there for a long time. Eventually he rose to his feet and clasped Herbert to his breast. 'Do not be anxious, dear brother,' Cuthbert whispered; 'God will answer our prayer.' Later that day Herbert left Cuthbert; and within a few weeks he had contracted a disease of the lungs, which – to his delight – he knew was terminal.

11.16 Return to Farne

By Christmas of the year 686 Cuthbert knew that death was close. He had been bishop for less than two years, and throughout that time had continued to yearn for solitude. Now he decided to lay down the burdens of his office, and retire to Farne Island. Once free of earthly worries, he hoped to devote the remaining months of his life to prayer, preparing himself for death. When the celebrations of Christmas were over, he made a final tour of his diocese, bidding farewell to all the faithful. Wherever he went people flocked to see him, many in tears at the prospect of his imminent death. Despite his own physical weakness, he sought to heal those who were sick and encourage those in mental distress. After his final tour he returned to Lindisfarne, where the monks gathered to hear his final words of guidance. Afterwards, they followed him down to the landing-stage, where a boat was ready to take him on his final earthly journey. All were sobbing. As Cuthbert was climbing into the boat, an old monk – who was strong in faith, but whose body had wasted away from dysentery – asked him: 'When may we expect to see you again?' Cuthbert replied: 'When you bring me back as a corpse.'

11.17 Final Illness

For two months after his arrival at Farne Island Cuthbert was able to enjoy again the delights of solitude, fitting his mind and body into the old routine. Then he fell ill. He felt as if a blazing fire was burning deep inside him, consuming his internal organs. On the day the illness struck a monk from Lindisfarne called Herefrith was visiting Cuthbert; and the following day Herefrith rowed back to Lindisfarne, to fetch other monks. This small group nursed Cuthbert, meeting all his physical needs; and they listened to him, eager to hear any words of wisdom from their dying leader. Each morning Herefrith came to Cuthbert's hut to see his condition; and over a period of three weeks Herefrith observed the disease getting worse. Then one morning Cuthbert ordered Herefrith and the other monks to return to Lindisfarne, so that he could have a few more days of solitude. Herefrith begged Cuthbert to let them stay, and continue looking after him; but Cuthbert was adamant. 'When should we come back?' Herefrith asked. 'When God wants,' Cuthbert replied. 'He will show you.' Herefrith and his companions rowed back to Lindisfarne. As soon as they landed, a terrible storm arose which lasted for five days, making the sea between Lindisfarne and Farne Island too rough to cross. Throughout that time a rota of monks was organised, so prayers could be said for Cuthbert in Lindisfarne church day and night.

11.18 Herefrith's Care

Finally the storm abated, and Herefrith and his companions decided to row back to Farne Island. When they arrived, they found Cuthbert sitting in the guest house near the landing stage, as if he were expecting them. Herefrith rushed in to see his condition. One of his feet, which had been swollen for a long time, had developed an ulcer. Herefrith warmed some water and bathed the foot. Then he gave him some warm wine. Cuthbert was now very weak, with almost no flesh on his body. 'What have you been eating while we have been away?' Herefrith asked. Cuthbert showed Herefrith a few small onions. 'Whenever my mouth was parched and my body was sweating with fever,' Cuthbert replied, 'I cooled myself with these.' 'And what have you been doing during these past five days?' Herefrith persisted. Cuthbert sighed, as if he were weary of these queries. Then he said: 'When you left I came in here to the guest house, and I have stayed here. I wanted you to find me easily when you returned.' 'But we could have come to your hut, and found you there,' said Herefrith. 'I have never allowed anyone to enter my hut,' Cuthbert replied. Then in a whisper he added: 'While I have been waiting here, the devil has attacked me with greater force than ever before. But in God's strength I have defeated him.'

11.19 Argument about Burial Arrangements

Herefrith carried Cuthbert back to his hut, and laid him on the bed. This was the first time that Cuthbert had allowed another person into his hut. The following morning Herefrith came to the hut again to see if Cuthbert's condition had worsened overnight. Cuthbert beckoned Herefrith to his bedside. 'When I am dead,' Cuthbert said, 'I want you to bury my body to the south of the oratory, beside the cross which I erected there. Many years ago an abbot called Cudda gave me a stone coffin which you will find under the turf on the north side of the oratory. And inside the coffin you will find a linen cloth given to me by an abbess called Verca. Wrap my body in the cloth, and then put my body in the coffin. Afterwards carry the coffin to the burial-place.' 'I ask you,' said Herefrith, 'to allow us to carry your body back to Lindisfarne, to be buried near your brethren'. 'I wish to be buried' replied Cuthbert, 'where I have fought spiritually for the Lord. Besides it will be far less trouble for you if I am buried here. Although I am a sinner, many people foolishly regard me as a saint. So if I am buried at Lindisfarne, you will be flooded with visitors coming to my grave. And they will disturb the peace of the monastery.' Herefrith was not persuaded by this argument, insisting that the brethren would not find the presence of his body irksome, since they would regard welcoming visitors as a privilege. 'If you go against my wishes,' concluded Cuthbert, 'I suggest that you bury my body inside the church. Then the brethren may visit my grave whenever they wish; and they will be able to control the numbers of visitors who can do so.'

11.20 Final Instructions

When Cuthbert realised that death was imminent, he asked to be carried to the oratory. He was now extremely weak, and he found it hard even to speak. Herefrith asked him if he would give some final words of counsel to the brethren who were on the island. Cuthbert nodded, and Herefrith summoned the whole group. In a hoarse whisper Cuthbert began to speak: 'In your monastery, as in every community, the people are mainly good; their intentions are benign and their hearts are kind. But in every soul there is an element of pride; and this can do incalculable damage, causing grievous disputes and destroying every semblance of brotherhood. So always be on your guard against that element of pride within your own soul, never allowing it to infect your words and actions; then ultimately it will shrivel up. And be vigilant against the effects of pride within your community. Do not be afraid to criticise the words and actions of others which are prompted by pride – while at the same time expressing your love for those you rebuke. In this way the King of Love will reign in your community, bringing peace and harmony to every aspect of your common life.'

11.21 Teaching on a Common Spirit

'When in the monastery you gather together to discuss matters of common concern,' Cuthbert continued, 'let your aim always be to reach unanimity. Reaching unanimity not only preserves harmony and good will within the brotherhood; it is also a test that God's Holy Spirit has guided your decisions. When people come to you seeking hospitality, never turn them away nor treat them with contempt. Welcome them warmly, and provide them with food and shelter, treating them as though they belonged to your community. Thus by your actions you will be proclaiming Christ's gospel to them. Do not regard yourselves as superior to those brothers who have difficulty in keeping the monastic rule; in God's eyes merit lies not in a person's ability to keep the rule, but in their good intentions and sincere efforts to keep it. Remember that even the holiest saint amongst you remains vulnerable to evil influences. Thus if one of your brethren, or a guest, starts to sow the seeds of discord and doubt amongst you, expel that person at once, before the seeds can germinate and grow.'

11.22 Final Communion and Death

As Cuthbert spoke his voice grew steadily weaker, and the pauses between each sentence and phrase grew longer. His final words concerned the dangers of schism in the Church: 'In my lifetime there have been many disputes and divisions, even on this remote island. Some have favoured the customs practised by our spiritual father Columba; others have favoured the Catholic customs brought to us from Rome. This matter has now been settled, and we must also submit to the customs of the universal Church. Never again must Christian people on this island fall out on such matters; let us always live in unity.' He finished speaking in the early afternoon, and he lay quietly in the oratory until it was time for evening prayers. The monks gathered round him, and Herefrith gave him the bread and wine of Communion. Then he raised his eyes towards heaven, and stretched out his arms as if to embrace his Saviour. His gaunt face broke into a smile, and the breath went from his body. Herefrith immediately lit two candles and carried them up the cliff above the oratory. This was the sign, agreed in advance, telling the monks of Lindisfarne that Cuthbert had died. The monk standing on Lindisfarne watch-tower saw the candles, and rushed down to the church where the monks were already assembled. The monks spent the night giving thanks to God for Cuthbert's life on earth.

Part 12

John:
the Healer of Beverley

12.1 Ministry at Hexham

John was born near Beverley, to the east of York, and became a monk at Hilda's monastery in Whitby. He was respected by all his brethren for his holiness and devotion. In the year of our Lord 687 he was appointed Bishop of Hexham. During his time at Hexham he spent every Lent with a few companions in an isolated house about a mile and a half from the town. The house stood in the middle of an ancient burial-ground, and was surrounded by woodland. There he and his companions would pray and read the Scriptures. Each year John invited someone who was seriously ill or disabled to join them, in the hope that their prayers would effect a cure. Thus one Lent a young man came who was completely dumb, and whose head was covered with scabs and scales so that his hair never grew. On the second Sunday of Lent John asked the young man to stick out his tongue; and John made the sign of the cross on it. John then asked the boy to say something; and the boy uttered the word 'Yes.' John now asked the boy to repeat the letters of the alphabet after him. By the end of the day the boy was pronouncing whole sentences; and throughout the following night the boy was so overjoyed at the gift of speech, that he did not stop talking and singing until dawn. Through the rest of Lent John frequently laid his hands on the boy's head. By Easter the scales and scabs had gone, and the boy had a full head of hair. John invited the boy to become a monk; but the boy preferred to return home and serve his family.

12.2 Healing of a Young Nun

In the year of our Lord 705 Wilfred became Bishop of Hexham, and John moved to the bishopric of York. His birth-place, Beverley, fell within the boundaries of his diocese. He decided to found a monastery there; and a short distance away at Watton he founded a convent, installing a woman of exceptional holiness, called Heriberg, as abbess. The whole area is covered in dense woodland. On one occasion when John was visiting the convent Heriberg told him that one of her nuns, called Coenburg, was seriously ill, suffering a violent pain in her arm. Heriberg begged John to come and bless the nun, and also to lay hands upon her. 'This young nun is especially dear to me,' Heriberg explained, 'since I want her to become abbess in my place.' So John went into Coenburg's cell, where she was writhing in agony. Her arm was now swollen to twice its normal size. John said a prayer over her; then he gently touched her arm, and blessed it. Some hours later when John was resting Heriberg rushed into his room: 'Coenburg wants you to come back to her cell at once,' Heriberg exclaimed. When John arrived, Coenburg was sitting up in her bed with a smile on her face. 'I would like you to share a drink with me,' Coenburg said. As she and John drank wine together, Coenburg explained that when John touched her arm, the pain seemed to go from her arm into his fingers; and as he left her cell, the pain went with him. Over the next few days the swelling gradually subsided, and Coenburg's arm was returned to its normal size. I can testify to the truth of this story, because I accompanied John on this visit.

12.3 New Churches around York

John encouraged the nobles and squires in his diocese to build churches on their lands, to enable the local people to gather each Sunday for worship. When a church was complete, John visited it, and conducted a service dedicating it to God. About two miles from Beverley a squire called Puch built a magnificent church, which John came to dedicate. After the service Puch invited John to dine with him. At first John refused. But Puch explained that his wife had been seriously ill for forty days, and he wished John to come and heal her. John then took some of the holy water which he had blessed in the church. When they arrived at Puch's house, John instructed Puch's wife to drink half the water, and to apply the rest as a lotion to her body. John and Puch then went to dine. A few moments after they had sat down at the table Puch's wife appeared, carrying the dishes of food; and throughout the meal she served the food and drink. Puch could hardly believe his eyes. From that time until now Puch's wife has enjoyed perfect health.

12.4 Healing of a Boy

As John's reputation as a healer spread throughout his diocese, people from every village urged him to come and cure those who were sick. John was unable to accept all these invitations; and the only way the people could be sure of a positive response was to build a church, and ask him to dedicate it. A squire called Addi, in a remote part of the diocese, had a boy who suffered paralysis in all his limbs, so that he could hardly move. Addi built a church, and invited John to come and dedicate it. By the time the church was complete and John arrived, Addi and all his family were convinced that the boy was about to die. After the services of dedication Addi invited John to visit the boy. When John entered the room he found that the boy's coffin had already been made, and had been placed beside his bed. Everyone present was in tears. John said a prayer over the boy and blessed him. Then he left the room, saying 'Hurry up, lad, and get well.' About an hour later John sat down to dinner with Addi and his family. During the meal the boy sent a message to Addi saying that he was thirsty, and asking for a drink. Addi was delighted that the boy could now drink. He poured wine into a cup and asked John to bless it. When the wine was brought into the boy's room, those attending him lifted the cup to his lips. As soon as he took a sip his limbs began to move, and he clasped the cup in his own hands. Then he climbed out of bed, walked to the dining-hall, knelt down at John's feet, and thanked him. John invited the boy to join them at table and make merry.

12.5 Heribald's Accident

Wherever he went, John always took with him young men who felt called to the priesthood. He trained them for this office both by his words and by his example. On one occasion John was riding with a group of these young men along a remote lane. They reached a stretch of flat open countryside suitable for galloping; and the young men asked John's permission to have a race. At first John refused, saying that such activities are unprofitable. The young men persisted, and John relented. But he added: 'Heribald must not take part; his constitution is too frail.' As the others galloped ahead, Heribald stayed behind, sulking at John's prohibition. After about a minute Heribald could no longer restrain himself: he spurred his horse, and raced at full speed towards his friends. Across the path lay a large boulder, which Heribald did not see; the horse jumped, and sent Heribald through the air. When he landed he crushed his arm and cracked his skull. John and the other young men rushed over to help Heribald. They carried him to a nearby cottage, and John spent the whole of the following night at Heribald's side, praying for his recovery. Heribald lay motionless, as if he were dead. Then as dawn broke, Heribald opened his eyes. 'Who am I?' asked John. 'You are my beloved bishop,' Heribald replied. 'Since my fall, I have felt your prayers strengthening me. You are saving my life.'

12.6 Heribald's Recovery

After Heribald had regained consciousness, John laid his hands on Heribald's cracked skull and blessed him; then John continued to pray silently at the bedside. A few hours later John spoke again: 'Heribald, have you been baptised?' 'Yes,' replied Heribald, 'I have been washed in the waters of salvation.' 'Who was the priest who ordained you?' John asked. Heribald gave the name. 'I fear', said John, 'that you were not validly baptised. That man was so lazy that, when people came to him seeking baptism, he never bothered to teach them the faith. So I ordered him to cease his priestly ministry.' Immediately John began to teach Heribald the basic tenets of the Christian faith. He then put a bandage on Heribald's skull, and carried him to a nearby church. John filled the font with water, and baptised Heribald. For many years afterwards Heribald was always at John's side, assisting him in every aspect of his work. In 717 John decided that he was too old to continue as a bishop. So he resigned his office, and retired to the monastery he had founded at Beverley, spending the last four years of his life there. He was buried in the porch of the monastery church.

Part 13

Wilbrord and the Hewalds:
the Gospel in Frisia

13.1 *Egbert's Abortive Mission*

The first person to preach the gospel in Frisia was Wilfred. He was sailing from Britain to Gaul, with the intention of travelling to Rome, when a strong westerly wind blew his boat to the estuary of the Rhine. As winter was approaching he was compelled to spend the winter there. But although many were impressed at his words, few offered themselves for baptism. The next to consider this task was a man of great holiness called Egbert. As a young man Egbert had gone to Ireland with Chad, where they became monks. Egbert stayed longer there than Chad. But eventually like Chad he came to believe that God was calling him to spread the gospel amongst the heathen. He heard that across the sea there were many Germanic people, who were of the same stock as the Angles and Saxons who had settled in Britain. And since he himself belonged to the Anglo-Saxon nation, he decided to sail around Britain and take the gospel to these Germans. As soon as Egbert had made this decision, there were many signs indicating that the project would fail. In particular one monk at his monastery had a vision one night in which he received a message to pass on to Egbert. In the morning the monk took this message to Egbert: 'You are not to go on the journey you plan; instead you should sail to Iona, and instruct the monks there.' Egbert sensed that this message might be divine, but he continued to make preparations.

He built a boat, and filled it with enough food and drink for a long voyage; he then waited for a favourable wind; leaving the boat on the beach ready to launch. While he was waiting a storm sent violent waves up the beach, smashing the boat into pieces and ruining the provisions.

13.2 Wictbert's Failure

Amongst those who were intending to travel with Egbert to Frisia was a monk called Wictbert. Far from daunting him, Egbert's failure fanned Wictbert's desire to preach the gospel in Frisia. Wictbert had lived for some years as a hermit, when he had read deeply about every aspect of Christian doctrine; he was thus famous for his theological knowledge. He built a new boat, and with a few companions sailed safely to the mouth of the Rhine. He met the Frisian king, Radbod, who allowed him to travel freely, telling people about Jesus Christ. But after two years of hard work he had not won a single convert. He sailed back to Ireland, and resumed living as a hermit. Despite his own failure, and that of Wictbert, Egbert was still concerned about the salvation of the Frisians; and he looked for others who might be willing to preach the gospel to them. Eventually he found a remarkable young man called Wilbrord, who combined profound holiness with great eloquence and charm. Wilbrord's father had abandoned his family to live as a hermit near the mouth of the Humber; and before leaving, he had entrusted his son to the monks of Ripon. On reaching adulthood Wilbrord had yearned for a more austere way of life than Ripon offered, and – like Egbert some years previously – he travelled to Ireland in search of it. He joined a monastery; but after twelve years he became restless, longing to use his eloquence in God's service. Thus he responded with enthusiasm to Egbert's proposal.

13.3 Wilbrord's Success

Wilbrord sailed from Ireland and landed at the mouth of the Rhine in the year of our Lord 690. He walked to the city of Utrecht, where he found that Radbod – who had been king during Wictbert's unsuccessful mission – had been overthrown by a man called Pippin. Although Pippin was a heathen, he had heard many good reports about the Christian faith. So he welcomed Wilbrord warmly, and urged him to preach the gospel throughout Frisia; he also issued a decree, ordering that no one should hinder Wilbrord in his work. Pippin himself received baptism, and soon many others were following his example. After a time Wilbrord decided to travel to Rome, both to gain the Pope's approval for his mission, and to ask for relics of the Apostles and martyrs. His intention was to build churches throughout Frisia, and he wished to place these relics under the altars. The Pope was overjoyed to hear of Wilbrord's success, and gave him a large number of relics. Wilbrord then returned to Frisia, and with Pippin's support began to build churches in every part of the country. In 696 Pippin sent a letter to the Pope, asking him to consecrate Wilbrord as archbishop of Frisia. The Pope agreed, and invited Wilbrord back to Rome; at the service of consecration the Pope gave Wilbrord the name Clement. Wilbrord remained in Frisia for the rest of his life, continuing to preach the gospel. He died in 738 at the age of 80.

13.4 The Hewalds' Martyrdom

News of Wilbrord's success in Frisia reached Ireland, from where Wilbrord had sailed. And this inspired two other priests to follow his example. They were both called Hewald, but they were distinguished by the colour of their hair: so one was known as Hewald the Black, and the other as Hewald the White. Like Wilbrord and Egbert, they were English, and had travelled to Ireland to become monks. They were both devout and religious, but Hewald the Black was more learned in the Holy Scriptures. They sailed towards Frisia, but the wind blew them to the province of the Old Saxons, a short distance along the coast. The Old Saxons possess a unique political system. They do not have a king, but regard all the nobles as equal in status. Whenever war is imminent they cast lots, and the noble on whom the lot falls becomes commander of the whole army; but as soon as war ends, the nobles revert to equality. When the Hewalds landed, the manager of one of the nobles' estates saw them, and took them to his home, promising to introduce them to his lord in due course. The Hewalds spent their time singing psalms and praying; and each day they celebrated Holy Communion. When local people realised that the Hewalds belonged to a different religion, they became frightened, wondering if the Hewalds would convert their lord to their faith – and he in turn would foist it on his subjects. So one day they came to the manager's house and seized the Hewalds. They killed Hewald the White outright with a sword; they tortured Hewald the Black by slowly tearing off his limbs, until he bled to death. Then they threw their bodies in the river. When Pippin of Frisia heard what had happened, he sent priests from amongst his own people to preach to the Old Saxons.

Part 14

Biscop:
the Abbot of Wearmouth

14.1 First Visit to Rome

Biscop was born in the year of our Lord 628. His father was a Northumbrian nobleman, of Angle descent. As a boy Biscop had the grave and solemn manner of an old man, and was keenly interested in spiritual and religious matters. When he reached adulthood the king of Northumbria, Oswy, asked him to become an advisor. Biscop proved a loyal and valuable servant, promoting justice and equity throughout the kingdom. But by the age of twenty-five Biscop was convinced that God wanted him to be a monk; and he asked the king for permission to enter a monastery. Oswy responded by offering Biscop land on which to found a new monastery. Biscop said that, if he were to become the father of a new community, he must prepare himself both spiritually and mentally for this task. Thus he decided to travel to Rome, visiting monasteries both in the city itself and on the route there. At each monastery he would listen to the abbot and the brethren, and observe their way of life. Then he would return to Northumbria, to put into practice all he had learnt.

14.2 Lessons in Rome

Biscop went first from Northumbria to Kent. There he met

Wilfred, who also wished to visit Rome; and they decided to travel together. In addition to observing at close quarters many famous and illustrious monasteries, Biscop saw the tombs of the apostles Peter and Paul. He loved the sumptuous and magnificent acts of worship which he attended in Rome, as well as the architecture and decoration of the church buildings. He also called on the various libraries there, admiring the scholars who devoted their lives to reading old books and writing new ones. He quickly concluded that the Church in Rome, in all its different aspects, was the model, fashioned by God, which Churches throughout the world should imitate. Thus when Biscop returned to Northumbria he related to clergy and laity alike all he had seen and heard in Rome, trying to inspire them as he had been inspired. One of those who listened to Biscop with great interest was Alchfrid, the eldest son of King Oswy. Biscop now planned a second trip to Rome, in order to learn more; and he invited Alchfrid to accompany him. But Oswy was at this time quite hostile towards the Roman Church, preferring the old customs introduced to Britain by Columba. So he refused permission for Alchfrid to go to Rome; and Biscop made his second journey alone.

14.3 Second and Third Visits to Rome

Biscop arrived in Rome for the second time in the year of our Lord 666. And as before he took great delight in observing every detail of Roman religious practice. After a few months in Rome he judged himself ready to take monastic vows. He went to the monastery at Lérins, an island off the coast of southern Gaul, where he was warmly received. He spent two years there, following its rule in every detail; and during this time the abbot affirmed his vocation as a monk, giving him the name Benedict. At the end of this period he felt himself to be sufficiently well-versed in monastic life to lead a community in Britain. But before returning to his native land he decided to pay a further brief visit to Rome. Happily soon after he made this decision, a merchant ship called at Lérins on its way to Rome; so he was able to reach the beloved city very quickly by sea. When he landed he met Wighard, the monk whom Egbert, king of Kent, had sent to Rome to be consecrated as archbishop of Canterbury. And then, when Wighard died of the plague which was sweeping through Rome, Biscop assisted the Pope in finding another candidate. Having chosen Theodore to be archbishop, and Hadrian as his assistant, the Pope ordered Biscop to be their guide on the journey to Britain — and their interpreter when they arrived.

14.4 Fourth Visit to Rome

When Biscop landed in Kent with Theodore and Hadrian, King Egbert received them with great joy. Theodore was duly enthroned as archbishop, and he in turn appointed Biscop to take charge of the monastery at Canterbury. After two years there, Biscop felt he should now take up Oswy's proposal, of founding a new monastery in Northumbria. He wished this monastery to be a centre of scholarship. So he went to Rome for a fourth time to obtain books. His funds were limited, so he asked well-wishers in Rome to donate books or sell them to him at a favourable price. By this means he brought back a large number of books on all branches of theology. When he reached Northumbria he told Egfrid, who was now king, all that he had done since leaving home; and he asked Egfrid to support his ambition of bringing to his native land a pattern of monastic life based on what he had seen in Rome and Lérins. Egfrid was enthused with Biscop's plans, and immediately gave him a large area of land on which to build a monastery. This was on the north bank at the mouth of the River Wear. Biscop arrived at this site in the year of our Lord 674, accompanied by a small group of other monks.

14.5 The Church at Wearmouth

Biscop began by building a small wooden church, and huts for himself and his companions. The following year he crossed the sea to Gaul, to find masons who could build for him a stone church in the Roman style. A year later, in 676, they had already completed the gable ends. And when the church was nearly complete, he sent agents to Gaul to find glaziers – craftsmen who at that time were unknown in Britain – to put glass in the windows. The glaziers not only executed this task with great skill; they also taught a number of local people their skills. Those people then made glass lamps for the church. Biscop then ordered from Gaul and beyond the sacred vessels for the altar, and vestments for himself and the other monks to wear when they celebrated Mass. He thus created the most magnificent church in the whole of Britain. But even now he would not rest content. He loved to gather ornaments of every kind to put into the church, both from within Britain and from abroad. So the church soon contained an exceptional collection of artistic objects.

14.6 Fifth Visit to Rome

Once the community at Wearmouth had become established, Biscop set off on his fifth trip to Rome. And he returned with a greater variety of spiritual treasures than ever before. Firstly he had a huge quantity of books on a wide range of theological and secular subjects; thus the monastery library multiplied in size and scope. Secondly he had an abundant supply of relics of the apostles and martyrs, which he distributed to churches throughout Britain. Thirdly he had many pictures of the saints to put on the walls of the monastery church. These included portraits of the Virgin Mary and the twelve apostles which he hung over the central arch; scenes from the gospel stories which he hung on the south wall; and scenes from St John's

Apocalypse which he hung on the north wall. While he was in Rome on this occasion Biscop learnt how to chant and sing the psalms; and he brought back with him a cantor called John. This excellent singer became the choirmaster at Wearmouth, teaching all the monks there how to chant and sing. He also wrote down his instructions in a book, which he placed in the library for the benefit of future generations of monks. In addition Biscop obtained from the Pope a letter which guaranteed the monastery's independence, ensuring that it would remain free from external interference.

14.7 Foundation of Jarrow

The monastery at Wearmouth continued to grow not only in magnificence, but also in size; men from all over Britain flocked to join it. Egfrid was so impressed at Biscop's success that he granted another large area of land, adjoining the existing land, to support the monks. A year later, in the year of our Lord 682, Egfrid asked Biscop to found a second monastery at Jarrow. Egfrid recognized the danger that in due course the two communities could become rivals. Thus he stipulated that they should be bound together by ties of friendship and good will, with monks free to move from one to the other. Biscop chose seventeen monks from Wearmouth monastery to form the nucleus of the new foundation; and amongst them was Ceolfrid whom he appointed as their abbot. Ceolfrid had joined Biscop's community at Wearmouth at an early stage, and had accompanied him on one of his journeys to Rome. At the same time Biscop chose Eosterwine to be abbot at Wearmouth. By this means Biscop lifted from himself all practical responsibilities, so that he was free to travel even more extensively overseas collecting books and sacred objects.

14.8 Eosterwine's Ministry as Abbot

Eosterwine was Biscop's cousin. As a young man he became an officer in the Northumbrian army, quickly climbing to a high rank; and he led his troops with great skill and courage. But like Biscop he was indifferent to worldly honour. So when at the age of twenty-four he entered the monastery at Wearmouth, it never occurred to him to use his relationship with Biscop to his own advantage – and nor did Biscop show him special favour. He always saw himself as equal in every respect with the other monks; and the only matter in which he took pride was in keeping the monastic rule in every detail. At harvest time he helped with the winnowing and threshing; he took his turn in milking the ewes and the cows; he frequently assisted in baking bread and cooking the meals; and he worked hard in the vegetable and herb gardens. Eosterwine was aged only thirty when Biscop appointed him to abbot of Wearmouth; and Eosterwine accepted the office not because he regarded himself as worthy, but out of obedience to Biscop. As abbot he continued to share the manual work of the community; and whenever he was walking about the monastery, he offered to help the other brethren in whatever they were doing. He slept in the dormitory, rather than have a private room, and he ate the same food as everyone else. When a monk was falling short in some respect, Eosterwine persuaded him to mend his way with words of encouragement, rather than rebuke.

14.9 Sixth Visit to Rome

As soon as Eosterwine had taken charge of the monastery at Wearmouth, Biscop set off on his sixth journey to Rome. And he returned with even more sacred pictures than before. These included a number of pairs of pictures, painted one above the other on a board which showed how the Old Testament foreshadows the New. For instance, the first picture of one pair shows Isaac carrying the wood on which he was to be burnt as a sacrifice; the second picture shows Christ carrying the cross on which he was about to be crucified. In another pair the first picture shows Moses raising up the serpent in the desert; the second pictures shows the Son of Man being lifted up on the cross. Biscop also brought back from Rome two silk cloaks, woven and embroidered with incomparable skill. He did not want these cloaks for use within the monastery; rather he gave them to the king in exchange for more land. This proved to be Biscop's last visit to Rome. He was now an old man, and decided to devote the remaining years of his life to prayer and to meditation on the Scripture. His eyesight was failing, so a rota of young monks was arranged to come to his cell at hourly intervals and read a passage from the Bible.

14.10 The First Election

Biscop's final trip to Rome lasted three years. For the first two years Eosterwine, the man whom Biscop had appointed abbot of Wearmouth in his place, remained in good health. But then a plague swept across the region; and although Eosterwine was robust and strong, he succumbed to the disease and died. Once the worst pangs of grief had passed, the brethren held a meeting to discuss how a successor should be chosen. They found themselves confused and uncertain, so they decided that a small group should go to the new monastery at Jarrow, and ask the advice of its abbot Ceolfrid. Although Ceolfrid had himself been appointed by Biscop, he believed that in general the monks should elect their abbot. So he urged them to choose someone from their own community who excelled in humility, was free from all desire for power, possessed the highest moral character, and had a deep knowledge of the Scriptures. The monks returned to Wearmouth and reported Coelfrid's advice. So the brethren held a further meeting, at which they elected Sigfrid. This exceptional man had always rejected priestly orders, preferring to remain a deacon; and he suffered from a severe physical disability. This disability had enabled him to concentrate more fully on spiritual matters; and thus he fulfilled perfectly the criteria which Ceolfrid had specified. When Biscop returned from Rome he was both sad at the loss of his cousin Eosterwine, and filled with joy and admiration at how the brethren had responded.

14.11 Final Instructions

A year after his return from Rome for the last time Biscop began to suffer weakness in his limbs. This gradually worsened until his limbs were paralysed; and then the paralysis spread into his body, until only his lungs and his head were functioning properly. Knowing that he would soon depart this life, Biscop asked the brethren to assemble in the glorious church he had built. And in a hoarse whisper – his voice itself was almost paralysed – he gave his final instructions: 'Do not think that the rules I laid down for you when I founded this monastery were based on my own untutored ideas. During my frequent pilgrimages I visited seventeen monasteries in Rome and Gaul; and I stored in my mind all the wisdom that I learnt in those places. The way of life here at Wearmouth, and also at Jarrow, is thus a reflection of all that is best in the Christian world. Being a simple man,' he continued, 'I had to use my mind to store wisdom; but others who are far better educated can store wisdom in books, to be read by future generations. For this reason I have taken great pains to collect at Wearmouth books on every subject, sacred and secular. I ask you to keep this collection together, and not to distribute the books to other monasteries; thus people will be able to come to Wearmouth, and study here human wisdom in its totality. I also ask that you treat the books with great care, not letting them rot or decay.'

14.12 Teaching on Democracy

Biscop paused for a few minutes, sitting back in his chair to re-cover his breath. Then he continued his final speech to the monks of Wearmouth: 'You were right to elect an abbot to rule over you when Eosterwine died. The abbot is the servant of the community, and so should be chosen by the community. When deciding who is suitable to be abbot, do not be influenced by a person's social status or by his administrative abilities. Appoint someone who possesses moral strength and spiritual insight, and who is a good teacher of the gospel. Do not look outside the community for an abbot, but search among yourselves. I would rather that this monastery reverted to the wilderness it was before I arrived, than that it had an abbot who was chosen because of his father's rank. When one abbot dies or resigns, talk openly amongst yourselves in a spirit of humble honesty about who should succeed him. Strive to come to a common mind. Then, when you have chosen the new abbot, ask the bishop to come and bless him.'

14.13 A Dying Scene

By the time Biscop spoke to his brethren for the last time, Sigfrid, the man who the monks had elected as their abbot, had also fallen ill. And it was soon clear that he too would soon die. One day, as they both lay in their cells, they each expressed a desire to see the other. So two young monks put Sigfrid on a stretcher and carried him to Biscop's cell. They put the stretcher next to Biscop's bed, and lifted Sigfrid onto Biscop's bed, so their two heads rested on the same pillow. They were both so weak that they could only speak in whispers; thus by putting Sigfrid so close to Biscop the two young monks enabled the two old monks to converse. During this conversation Biscop and Sigfrid discussed the future of the twin monasteries of Wearmouth and Jarrow. And they decided to recommend to the two communities that, in addition to their own abbots, they also elect an abbot to oversee them both, ensuring that the close bands of friendship and mutual support are maintained. After Biscop and Sigfrid had finished speaking, a dozen monks entered Biscop's cell. Six of them stood on one side of the bed, and six on the other; and they sang psalms, the two groups chanting alternate verses. Sigfrid died two months after this episode. Biscop lingered for a further four months, unable to move or speak. He finally died during a cold January night, sixteen years after founding the monastery at Wearmouth.

Part 15

Ceolfrid:
the Abbot of Jarrow

15.1 *Early Years at Ripon*

Ceolfrid was the son of a Northumbrian nobleman. But rather than enjoy the material privileges of his birth, he decided to become a monk. He entered the monastery at Ripon, which Wilfred had founded; and he was ordained priest there at the early age of twenty-seven. He possessed great intelligence, and immersed himself in books of theology, so that he became one of the most learned men in Britain. But he was also an excellent cook; and for this reason the abbot of Ripon put him in charge of the monastery kitchens. The abbot, however, allowed him to travel to Canterbury, to study the books which the monastery there had collected; and on his return journey, he went to the monastery at Iken, to meet its remarkable founder Botolph. Biscop had known Ceolfrid as a boy, and knew of his reputation at Ripon for both theological knowledge and practical skill. So he invited Ceolfrid to join him at his new foundation in Wearmouth. Ceolfrid responded with enthusiasm; and a few months later Biscop appointed him as prior, to take charge of the monastery while Biscop was on a trip to Rome. Some of the monks resented Ceolfrid's rapid elevation, refusing to obey him. Ceolfrid became so distressed by this that he returned to Ripon. But on his return from Rome, Biscop persuaded Ceolfrid to return to Wearmouth.

15.2 Appointment at Jarrow

Despite his noble birth and great intelligence, Ceolfrid was a humble man who took no pleasure in exercising authority over others. From the moment he entered monastic life, he had no other desire than to keep the monastic rule, and to praise God in song and in prayer. When he returned to Wearmouth, the monks who resented him gradually came to realise that their attitude was wrong; and they embraced him as a true spiritual brother. Thus in 682, when the king of Northumbria asked Biscop to start a twin monastery at Jarrow, it was clear to everyone that Ceolfrid was the ideal man to be abbot. Biscop duly appointed him to this office, and the bishop confirmed the appointment. Seventeen monks from Wearmouth volunteered to move with Ceolfrid to Jarrow; and together they set about building a church in which to worship, and huts in which to live. But soon afterwards a terrible calamity befell this new community: a plague descended upon it, killing all the brethren except two. The survivors were Ceolfrid himself, and a boy (Bede) who was being educated at the monastery. Nonetheless Ceolfrid, with the boy's assistance, continued the daily rhythm of worship; and soon God sent more young men to replenish the community.

15.3 Appointment as Abbot of Jarrow and Wearmouth

When Biscop died in the year of our Lord 689, the monks of Wearmouth and Jarrow gathered, as Biscop had advised, to elect an abbot of both monasteries. By this time Ceolfrid had been abbot of Jarrow for seven years, and had proved himself to be a man of energy, courage, acute and mature judgement, as well as being devout. The monks of Jarrow warmly commended him as suitable for this higher office; and the older monks at Wearmouth, who had known Ceolfrid during his time there, were equally keen. Thus by unanimous consent Ceolfrid was chosen. He ruled the two monasteries for twenty-eight years, treating them as a single community with two locations. He shared Biscop's ambition to make Wearmouth and Jarrow beacons of spiritual light, shining across Northumbria, Britain and beyond. His radiant personality attracted young men of every social class to join the monasteries, so that by the time of his death there were over six hundred members. To provide adequate space for both communal worship and private prayer, he built several new chapels. He persuaded the noblemen of Northumbria and elsewhere to donate Communion plate and vestments. He also asked for gifts of money which he used to buy books. Within the monasteries he arranged for many of the monks to learn the art of writing, so that they could copy sacred books. By making copies and by purchasing books from outside, Ceolfrid doubled the size of the libraries in both places.

15.4 Spiritual Teaching

Ceolfrid never tired of telling his brethren that the Scriptures should be their guide in all things. In order to make the Scriptures more readily available, he asked for three copies to be made of the entire Bible, each copy bound within a single volume. One of these copies was placed in Wearmouth library, another in Jarrow library, and the third was sent as a gift for the Pope. Ceolfrid practised what he taught, making the Scriptures his own abbot. As a result he acquired great spiritual authority, enabling him to restrain those who were sowing seeds of disharmony, and to nurture the seed of love in every soul. This inner spiritual authority also made Ceolfrid very honest with himself, so that he could see clearly his own weaknesses and limitations, as well as his strengths. He frequently referred to his advancing years, saying that, when he felt himself unable to fulfill his duties as abbot to the highest standards, he would willingly retire. No one imagined that such a time would come.

But as the years passed, the prospect of retirement, and thence of making a pilgrimage to Rome, seemed increasingly attractive. He turned the matter over in his mind for a long time, praying for divine guidance. Then in the spring of 716 he announced his retirement to his brethren, urging them to elect from amongst themselves a successor. And he added that, a soon as a new abbot was appointed, he would set off for Rome.

15.5 Last Communion

At first the monks of Wearmouth and Jarrow unanimously opposed Ceolfrid's plan to retire. One by one they came to his cell and fell on their knees, begging him to remain as their spiritual father. But he was adamant, ordering them to hold an election for his successor as quickly as possible. He was anxious to leave for Rome within a few weeks. This was partly because he feared that news of his intentions would leak out, inducing the Northumbrian king and nobles to come and urge him to stay. It was also because he knew that his time on earth was short, so any delay would increase the chance of his dying on the journey. Thus on 5 June he celebrated Communion for the last time with his brethren. The service took place at the church in Wearmouth, with the monks from both monasteries in attendance. After everyone had received the sacraments, Ceolfrid went to all the monks in turn, asking to be forgiven for any wrong he may have done in the past. Most of the monks were overcome with emotion, so that they could not speak; they simply nodded their heads. Then Ceolfrid gave each monk the kiss of peace.

15.6 Departure and Death

When he had kissed all his brethren, Ceolfrid walked out of the church and down to the sea where a boat was waiting for him.

The monks followed, singing a litany, but the words were frequently drowned out by the sound of sobbing. At the shore the monks fell to their knees, praying for God's mercy both on their beloved abbot, and on their community without him. Ceolfrid climbed into the boat, and the oarsmen began to row. The boat crossed safely to Gaul, and Ceolfrid began to ride southwards. He adhered strictly to the monastic pattern of prayer. He stopped his horse at exactly the same times during the day as the monks at Jarrow and Wearmouth were entering the church. He climbed down, and knelt down by the side of the road. He then prayed and recited the psalms at the same speed and rhythm as was used in church. Sadly however, Ceolfrid's final ambition was not fulfilled. He reached Langres in the Burgundy on the morning of 25 September. Almost immediately he fell ill, and died in the late afternoon; he was aged seventy-four. He was buried the following day in a monastery to the south of the city. Although the monks there had not known him, they sensed that he had been a man of exceptional holiness; and they wept at his funeral as if he had been their own spiritual father,

15.7 Hwaetberht's Election

After Ceolfrid's departure the monks at Wearmouth and Jarrow gathered in Wearmouth church. They prayed for divine guidance and then began discussing what they should do. They decided to elect a new abbot on the following Sunday, which was Pentecost; in the meantime they would fast, and ask God for guidance. When they gathered on Pentecost Sunday, they unanimously chose Hwaetberht as their abbot. Hwaetberht had been sent to Wearmouth as a child to be educated, and on reaching adulthood had taken monastic vows; so his mind and spirit were wholly immersed in the discipline and culture of monastic life. And from his earliest years he had been an adept pupil of the various monastic arts: writing, chanting, reading and teaching. He had also spent a substantial time in Rome, copying sacred books to bring back to Wearmouth and Jarrow. As soon as Hwaetberht was elected, a messenger was sent across the sea to catch up with Ceolfrid and tell him the news. The messenger found Ceolfrid a few miles north of Langres, only a week before Ceolfrid's death. When the messenger told Ceolfrid the news, Ceolfrid replied simply: 'Thanks be to God.'

Epilogue

The Death of Bede:
By a Disciple

1 *Teaching on Death*

During the fortnight prior to Easter, in the year of our Lord 735, Bede became increasingly weak, and his breathing grew heavier; but happily the pain of his illness lessened. From Easter until Ascension Day he was cheerful and happy, giving thanks to God for the many blessings he had enjoyed during the course of his life. Each day he gave us a lesson. And in his cell he recited the monastic offices at the same time as the rest of us were saying the offices in church. During the nights he prayed and sang psalms, except when sleep overcame him. His arms were almost continually outstretched, in a posture of thankfulness to God. Indeed I can truthfully affirm that I have never known anyone so filled with gratitude as Bede. During our lessons he frequently spoke about death. He liked to quote the saying of the apostle Paul: 'It is a fearful thing to fall into the hands of the living God.' He also sang one of our native Northumbrian songs whose words mean: 'Before setting out on that inevitable journey, the wise person reflects on what good and evil he has done, and what judgement his soul will receive after the body has died.' These words frightened us; so to give us comfort he sang the song for Ascension Day: 'King of glory, Lord of might, who on this day ascended in triumph above all heavens, do not leave us orphaned, but send to us the Spirit of truth. Alleluia.' And when he reached the words 'do not leave us orphaned', he broke down and wept.

2 Completion of His Work

During the final weeks of his life, in addition to giving lessons to his students and giving thanks to God, Bede was struggling to complete two important books. The first was extracts from the works of Isidore of Seville. The second was a translation into our own native language of the Gospel of St John. By the Tuesday before Ascension Day his breathing had become so laboured that he had to pause between each sentence. But he continued to dictate hour after hour, saying from time to time: 'Let us be quick. I do not know how long I can continue, because the Lord may call me quite soon.' That night Bede resisted sleep, and instead carried on dictating and praying. When dawn broke on Wednesday the pace of his dictation was faster than ever. At nine o'clock in the morning the monk who was taking dictation said to Bede: 'You have not yet translated the final chapter of St John's Gospel. But I do not want you to take any further trouble – you must rest.' 'It is no trouble,' Bede answered; 'go and sharpen your pen so you can write more quickly.' So for a further three hours Bede dictated, and the monk wrote down what he heard.

3 Completion of His Life

At midday Bede said to the young monk who was taking dictation: 'In that casket over there, in the corner of my cell, I have a few articles of value, such as pepper, linen and incense. Go quickly and fetch some of the senior monks, so that I can hand over to them these things which God has given me.' In great distress the young monk did as Bede asked. When the senior monks arrived, Bede gave them the contents of the casket. Then he begged them to pray for God's mercy on his soul. 'It is now time', he said, 'for my soul to be set free from this decaying body. I have had a long life, during which God has blessed me greatly. But now I long to see Christ my King in the fullness of his beauty.' The senior monks stayed with Bede for the rest of the day, talking about all sorts of spiritual matters. The atmosphere in Bede's cell was both joyful and sad. Then as dusk fell, the young monks who had been taking dictation said to Bede: 'Master, there is one sentence of your translation of St John's Gospel still unfinished.' Bede dictated the final sentence. After a pause the young monk said: 'It is finished.' 'You have spoken truly,' Bede replied; 'it is well finished. Now put your arms under my head, and lift me up, so I can see the place in my cell where I used to pray.' The young monk lifted Bede's head, and Bede chanted in a low whisper: 'Glory be to the Father, and to the Son, and to the Holy Spirit.' Then he breathed his last.

Appendix 1

The Main Figures

Aidan (d. 651) Monk of Iona. At King Oswald's invitation, led the mission to the Northumbrians. He founded the monastery at Lindisfarne.

Alban (d. c. 254) First British martyr. He was executed for his faith during the Roman occupation. He lived and died in Verulanium, which was later re-named after him.

Alchfrid Son of King Oswy of Northumbria. He strongly supported Wilfred in promoting Roman forms of Christianity. Although Alchfrid was the eldest son, Oswy nominated his second son Egfrid as successor.

Aldfrid (d. 704) King of Northumbria, after Oswy and Egfrid. He allowed Wilfred to return as Bishop of York, but later expelled him.

Augustine (d. c. 604) The first bishop of Canterbury. He was chosen by Pope Gregory to lead a mission to Britain. He enjoyed considerable success in Kent, under King Ethelbert and Queen Bertha, but failed to persuade the existing British Christians to accept his authority.

Bertha (d. c. 615) The queen of Kent, married to King Ethelbert. She was from the Frankish royal house, and was brought up as a Christian. On Augustine's arrival in Kent, she encouraged her husband to embrace Christianity.

Biscop (d. 689) The founder of the twin monasteries of Wearmouth and Jarrow. He travelled frequently to Rome, collecting books, relics and other treasures. He took the name Benedict on taking monastic vows.

Boisil (d. *c.* 661) The prior of Melrose. He welcomed Cuthbert into the monastery. He prophesied Cuthbert's future eminence.

Caedmon (d. 680) A monk at Whitby under Hilda. He was a herdsman who discovered in himself a divine gift for song. With Hilda's encouragement he put the Biblical stories into verse.

Cedd (d. 664) A monk at Lindisfarne, who was sent by King Oswy to lead a mission to the East Saxons. He was strongly supported by Sigbert, the local king, and made the old Roman fort of Othona his base. He also preached in Mercia, and founded the monastery at Lastingham.

Ceolfrid (d. 716) The first abbot of Jarrow, appointed by Biscop the founder. He later became abbot of Wearmouth and Jarrow which he treated as a single community.

Chad (d. 672) A monk from Lindisfarne. He was invited by King Wulfhere to lead a mission to Mercia. He made Lichfield his base. Earlier in his life he had lived in Ireland as a hermit, alongside Egbert.

Coenburg A nun at Watton, near Beverley. She was cured of a violent pain in her arm by John of Beverley.

Coifi The chief priest in York of the old pagan religion. He advised King Edwin to accept the Christian faith.

Colman (d. 676) A monk from Iona. He was successor to Aidan and Finan at Lindisfarne. He led the Celtic side at the Synod of Whitby. After his defeat, he and a group of followers retreated to Ireland, to maintain the Celtic traditions.

Columba (d. 597) The founder of the monastery of Iona. He was born in Ireland, where he founded a number of monasteries; but he was expelled for political reasons in 563, and crossed to Britain with twelve companions. He led missions to the Picts and Scots.

Cuthbert (d. 687)   Prior at Melrose, where he entered monastic life. He later moved to Lindisfarne. In both places he undertook extensive missionary work amongst the local people. He became a hermit on Farne Island, but was recalled to be bishop of the Northumbrian people.

Eadbald (d. 640)   King of Kent, succeeding his father Ethelbert who was Augustine's patron. He was initially hostile to Christianity, but later adopted the faith.

Eanfled (d. c. 704)   Daughter of King Edwin. She was baptised as a baby by Paulinus – the first baptism in York. After her father's death she went to live in Kent, where she was imbued with the Roman style of Christianity. She later returned north to marry King Oswy of Northumbria, and was Wilfred's patron.

Earconwald (d. 693)   Bishop to the East Saxons. He founded monasteries at Chertsey and Barking. He acquired a reputation for healing people.

Earpwald   King of the East Angles. He adopted Christianity through the influence of his friend King Edwin. But he failed to persuade his nobles to follow, and he was murdered by a pagan priest.

Ebba (d. 683)   The abbess of the monastery at Coldingham in Northumbria. She was aunt to King Egfrid. When Etheldreda, who was married to Egfrid, ran away, Ebba welcomed her.

Edwin (d. 632)   King of Northumbria, with his capital in York. He married Ethelburga, a Christian princess from Kent. She brought with her Paulinus, who persuaded Edwin and his nobles to embrace Christianity.

Egbert (d. 729) Monk of Iona. He lived for a period as a hermit in Ireland, alongside Chad. He led an abortive mission to Frisia, which stimulated a successful mission by Wictbert.

Egfrid (d. 685) King of Northumbria. He succeeded his father Oswy in 670. He married Etheldreda, who refused to consummate the marriage, and later ran away to found the convent at Ely. He expelled Wilfred from the bishopric of York, despite Archbishop Theodore's entreaties. But Theodore helped to make peace when Egfrid went to war against Ethelred of Mercia.

Egric (d. 635) King of the East Angles. He succeeded Sigbert when the latter entered a monastery. He dragged Sigbert out in order to encourage the East Angle troops in a battle against Penda of Mercia. But the East Angles lost, and both Egric and Sigbert were killed.

Eosterwine (d. 686) Abbot of Wearmouth, appointed by Biscop. As a young man he had been an officer in the Northumbrian army.

Ethelbert (d. 616) King of Kent. He welcomed Augustine, giving him a house in Canterbury. Later Augustine converted him to Christianity, and he became a staunch supporter of Augustine's mission.

Ethelburga (d. 675) Abbess of Barking. She was sister to Earconwald, the bishop of the East Saxons, and like him she acquired a reputation for healing.

Etheldreda (d. 679) Founder and abbess of Ely. The eldest daughter of Anna, King of the East Angles, she was required for political reasons to marry King Egfrid of Northumbria. She refused to consummate the marriage and eventually ran away, first to Coldingham where Egfrid's aunt Ebba was abbess; and then to Ely.

Ethelred King of Mercia. He came to the throne soon after

Chad's death. He conducted an especially cruel war against Kent.

Ethelwald Son of King Oswald of Northumbria. Oswald appointed him ruler of the southern part of his kingdom, Deira, with York as his capital. He invited Cedd to found a monastery in Deira.

Ethelwalh King of the South Saxons. He was converted to Christianity through the influence of King Wulfhere of Mercia. He then supported Wilfred's mission to his people.

Felix (d. 647) Missionary amongst the East Angles. Born in Gaul, King Sigbert invited him to East Anglia, where he established a monastery in Dunwich.

Finan (d. 661) Aidan's successor as abbot of Lindisfarne. He instructed Peada, ruler in Mercia, in the Christian faith and baptised him.

Fursey (d. 650) Missionary amongst the East Angles. Born in Ireland, he sailed to Britain in response to a dream. He landed at Burgh Castle, which he made his base.

Gregory (d. 604) Pope in Rome. He sent Augustine to Britain, and continued to guide Augustine's mission through letters.

Hadrian (d. 709) Assistant to Archbishop Theodore. As abbot of a monastery near Naples, he recommended Theodore to the Pope, and accompanied Theodore to Britain.

Herbert (d. 687) Hermit on an island in Derwentwater, in Cumbria. Cuthbert was his spiritual director.

Herewith Monk in Lindisfarne. He looked after the dying Cuthbert on Farne Island.

Heribald A young monk who was a disciple of John of Beverley. He was healed by John's prayers after falling from a horse.

Heriberg Abbess of the convent at Watton, near Beverley, appointed by John of Beverley, who founded the convent.

Hewald the Black and **Hewald the White** (d. *c.* 695) English monks who went to Frisia. They were captured and killed before they could begin their mission.

Hwaetberht (d. *c.* 747) Abbot of Wearmouth and Jarrow. Like Bede he was offered to the monastery as a child. He was elected abbot after Ceolfrid's departure for Rome.

Hilda (d. 680) Abbess of Whitby. The niece of King Edwin, she was baptised as a child with her uncle at York. She became a nun at Challes in Gaul, but was later invited by Aidan to lead a convent in Northumbria. She was abbess at Hartlepool before moving to Whitby. She was host to the Synod of Whitby, and patron of Caedmon.

John (d. 721) Bishop of York. Born near Beverley, he became a monk in Whitby. He was appointed Bishop of Hexham; and then moved to York, allowing Wilfred to come to Hexham. He gained a reputation as a healer. He encouraged local squires to build churches. And he founded two monastic communities, one for women at Watton, the other for men at Beverley.

Lucius (2nd century) British chieftain. He wrote to the Pope requesting instruction in the Christian faith. After instruction he and many of his followers were baptised. According to Bede they were the first native British Christians.

Mellitus (d. 624) Bishop of London. He came to Britain in 601 to assist Augustine. He was appointed bishop to the East Saxons, with London as his base with the support of King Sabert. But after Sabert's death he was expelled. He later became archbishop of Canterbury.

Offa (d. *c.* 709) King of the East Saxons. He abdicated, and followed Coenred, who had abdicated the throne of Mercia, to Rome, where both became monks.

Oswald (d. 642)   King of Northumbria. He succeeded his uncle Edwin. He invited the monks of Iona to preach the Christian faith in the kingdom.

Oswin (d. 651)   King of Deira, the southern region of Northumbria. He took power after Oswald's death, and was a friend and supporter of Aidan. He was murdered by Oswy.

Oswy (d. 670)   King of Northumbria. He initially took power in Bernicia, the northern region of Northumbria, but gained control of the whole kingdom by murdering Oswin. He convened the Synod of Whitby, and was won over by Wilfred's arguments in favour of Roman customs. He defeated and killed Penda of Mercia in battle.

Paulinus (d. 644)   Bishop of York. He came to Britain in 601 to support Augustine. When Ethelburga of Kent went to York to marry King Edwin, Paulinus accompanied her. He instructed Edwin and his nobles in the Christian faith, and baptised them. When Penda of Mercia killed Edwin in battle, Paulinus retreated south, and became Bishop of Rochester.

Peada (d. 656)   Son of Penda of Mercia. He became a Christian when he married the daughter of King Oswy of Northumbria. When Oswy defeated Penda, Oswy appointed him as governor of South Mercia; but he died six months later.

Penda (d. 655)   King of Mercia. He was highly successful in battle, defeating the East Angles and the Northumbrians under Edwin. He was indifferent to religion, looting and destroying churches. He was eventually defeated and killed by King Oswy of Northumbria.

Pippin   King of Frisia. He seized the throne from Radbod. He welcome Wilbrord, and was converted to Christianity by him.

Radbod King of Frisia. Although a heathen, he allowed Wictbert to preach freely.

Redwald (d. c. 620) King of East Anglia. He received baptism during a visit to Kent. But he failed to persuade his wife or others in East Anglia to follow his example.

Sabert (d. c. 616) Nephew of King Ethelbert of Kent, who appointed him to rule the East Saxons. He supported Mellitus as bishop of the East Saxons.

Sebbi (d. 694) King of the East Saxons. He supported Earconwald as bishop to his people.

Sexburg (d. c. 700) Abbess of Ely. Daughter of Anna, king of the East Angles and younger sister of Etheldreda, she took over the convent at Ely after Etheldreda's death.

Sigbert (d. c. 627) King of the East Angles. During a period of exile in Gaul, he met Felix. And when he became king, he invited Felix to lead a mission amongst his people.

Sigbert (d. c. 653) King of the East Saxons. He became a Christian through the influence of King Oswy of Northumbria. He asked Oswy to send a missionary to his people; and Oswy sent Cedd.

Sigfrid (d. 688) Abbot of Wearmouth. After the premature death of Eosterwine, the monks of Wearmouth elected Sigfrid as their abbot.

Theodore (d. 690) Archbishop of Canterbury. Greek by birth, he was sent by the Pope to take over the English Church soon after the Synod of Whitby. He successfully reformed the Church along Roman lines, establishing a code of canon laws, and also promoting scholarship.

Vortigern (5th century) British chieftain. He invited Angles and Saxons to protect his people from the Picts and Scots. The Angles and Saxons soon became the aggressors, conquering Britain for themselves.

Wictbert   Hermit in Ireland. Inspired by Egbert's abortive venture, he sailed to Frisia, where he preached the gospel. But his mission failed, and he returned after two years.

Wighard (d. 665)   Archbishop elect of Canterbury. Chosen by King Oswy and King Egbert as archbishop, he travelled to Rome to be consecrated by the Pope. But he died soon after arriving in Rome, prompting the Pope to appoint Theodore instead.

Wilbrord (d. 738)   Archbishop of Frisia. An eloquent preacher, he conducted a successful mission to Frisia, winning many converts, including King Pippin, and building numerous churches. At Pippin's request the Pope consecrated him as archbishop of the country.

Wilfred (d. 709)   Abbot of Ripon and Bishop of Hexham. Born in Northumbria, he became a monk in Lindisfarne. But after travelling to Rome, he became an ardent proponent of Roman customs. He was appointed Abbot of Ripon, and successfully led the Roman side at the Synod of Whitby. He was the next bishop of York, but was opposed successfully by King Oswy and King Egfrid, the latter expelling him. He led missions to Frisia and to the South Saxons. He finally returned to Northumbria as Bishop of Hexham.

Wulfhere (d. 675)   King of Mercia. Having avenged the defeat of his father Penda by King Oswy, he actively supported Christian missions in Mercia. He appointed Chad as Bishop of Mercia.

Appendix 2

The Main Places

Kent

The kingdom of Kent corresponded roughly to the modern county of Kent. The important places within Kent which Bede mentions are:

Canterbury   The capital city of the kingdom, where Ethelbert allowed Augustine to establish a monastery. Although Gregory intended that the archbishop of southern Britain should reside in London, the hostility of Londoners made this impossible. Thus by the time of Theodore's accession, Canterbury had been established as the seat of the archbishop. And persistent problems in York gave the archbishop of Canterbury effective jurisdiction right up to the Scottish border.

Rochester   Apparently the second most important town in Kent. In 604 Augustine established it as a separate diocese, installing Justus as its first bishop. The church was destroyed, and the bishop driven into exile, by Ethelred of Mercia.

Thanet   The tip of north-east Kent where Augustine and his companions landed. It was an island in that two rivers joined at its western boundary. Near it stood the old Roman fort of Reculver where later a monastery was built in honour of Augustine's mission.

Northumbria – Deira

The kingdom of Northumbria was divided into two provinces. The southern province was called Deira, and corresponded roughly to modern Yorkshire. The main places were:

Beverley A monastery founded by John, in the east of Deira. John established the monastery after he became Bishop of York. Later he retired and died there.

Hackness The retreat which Hilda established towards the end of her life. It lies to the south-west of Whitby.

Lastingham A monastery which Cedd founded and where he died in 659. The site was previously inhabited by robbers; but Cedd drove out the evil influence by prayer and fasting. Chad lived there as a monk until his appointment as Bishop of Mercia.

Ripon A monastery where Wilfred became abbot at the early age of 30. Alchfrid, who ruled Deira on behalf of his father Oswy, threw out the monks of Ripon because they followed the Celtic customs. He then appointed Wilfred to re-establish the community on Roman lines.

Watton A convent near Beverley, founded by John at the same time as he founded the monastery at Beverley itself. He appointed Heriburg as abbess, and cured a nun called Coenburg of a violent pain.

Whitby A monastery for men and women, founded by Hilda. It became a centre of scholarship, and was the venue of the great Synod. Caedmon was a cowherd there.

York The capital of Deira, which under King Edwin was capital of the whole of Northumbria. In Gregory's plan it was to be the seat of the archbishop for northern Britain, though in Bede's time persistent conflict prevented this.

Northumbria – Bernicia

The northern province of Northumbria, called Bernicia, corresponded roughly to the modern counties of Northumberland and Durham. The main places in Bede's time were:

Bamburgh The capital of Bernicia, which under King Oswald was the capital of the whole kingdom. It overlooks Lindisfarne on the Northumbrian coast. Aidan died near there.

Coldingham A convent ruled by Ebba, the aunt to King Egfrid. Etheldreda, Egfrid's wife, fled there when she decided to leave him.

Farne Island The largest of a group of rocky islands off the coast from Bamburgh and Lindisfarne. Cuthbert went there to be a hermit, and died there.

Hartlepool A convent on the coast south of Wearmouth, where at Aidan's request Hilda served as abbess.

Hexham A church on the River Tyne, which became the centre of a diocese. John of Beverley was an early bishop. But as part of a settlement allowing Wilfred to return to Northumbria, John was replaced by Wilfred.

Jarrow The second monastery founded by Biscop. It stands at the mouth of the Tyne. Coelfrid was the first abbot, and Bede spent most of his life there.

Lindisfarne A large island near Bamburgh, where Aidan established his monastery. It is connected to the mainland at low tide. Cuthbert was prior there, and numerous men of distinction trained there, including Chad, Cedd and Wilfred.

Melrose A monastery on the River Tweed. Cuthbert became a monk there, welcomed by the old prior Boisil.

Walton (or **Warbotte**) The village next to Hadrian's Wall where Peada, the Mercian prince, was baptised by Finan, abbot of Lindisfarne; and where Finan also baptised Sigbert, king of the East Saxons.

Wearmouth   The first monastery founded by Biscop on land given by King Egfrid. Along with Jarrow it became a great centre of learning, with a vast library built up by Biscop and Ceolfrid.

East Anglia

The kingdom of East Anglia corresponded approximately with the counties of Norfolk and Suffolk, and stretching into eastern Cambridgeshire. The major places were:

Burgh Castle   A Roman fort, converted into a monastery by Fursey. Overlooking the Yare estuary, it was one of a series of forts built by the Romans for protection against Anglo and Saxon invaders. By Fursey's time probably only the perimeter walls survived.

Dunwich   A thriving port where Felix established a monastery. In Bede's time it was the centre of the East Anglian Church. King Sigbert retired there. The site of the port and the monastery has since been washed away by the sea.

Ely   An island in the middle of the Fens, which at that time were a vast expanse of marshes and river. Etheldreda established her monastery there, which after her death was taken over by her sister Sexburg.

Essex

The territory of the East Saxons covered Essex, London and much of Surrey, as well as most of Hertfordshire. The main places were:

Barking   A monastery for men and women, founded by Earconwald. He made his sister Ethelburga the first abbess.

Chertsey A second monastery founded by Earconwald, on the banks of the River Thames. He himself made his home there.

Hatfield The site of the second council of bishops and priests called by Theodore. Its purpose was to resist the 'monophysite' heresy spreading into Britain.

Hertford The site of the first council called by Theodore. Its purpose was to pass a basic code of Church laws.

London The old Roman capital, which Gregory planned as the seat of the archbishop of southern Britain. Mellitus was appointed by Augustine as the first bishop but was later driven out.

Othona A Roman fort, built to repel Anglo and Saxon invaders. Cedd turned it into a monastery, where he trained men to go out and preach the gospel.

Verulamium The Roman city north of London where Alban lived and was martyred.

Bibliography

There are two good translations available of Bede's *A History of the English Church and People*:

SHERLEY-PRICE, LEO, Penguin 1955 (reprinted).

STEVENS, JOHN, J. M. Dent 1910 (reprinted).

There is also a good translation of Bede's *Life of Cuthbert* and *Lives of the Abbots of Wearmouth and Jarrow*:

WEBB, J. F. and FARMER, D. H., Age of Bede, Penguin 1965 (reprinted).

Index

References to the Original Texts

Part and Chapter in this book	Part and Chapter in *A History of the English Church and People*
1.1	1.1
1.2	1.1
1.3	1.2
1.4	1.3 1.4 1.5
1.5	1.6
1.6	1.7
1.7	1.7
1.8	1.7
1.9	1.7 1.8
1.10	1.11 1.12
1.11	1.14
1.12	1.14 1.15
1.13	1.15
2.1	2.1
2.2	2.1 1.23
2.3	1.25
2.4	1.25
2.5	1.26
2.6	1.26 1.27
2.7	1.28
2.8	1.29
2.9	1.30
2.10	1.31
2.11	1.32
2.12	2.2

Part and Chapter in this book	Part and Chapter in A History of the English Church and People			
2.13	2.2			
3.1	2.3	2.4		
3.2	2.5			
3.3	2.5			
3.4	2.7	2.8	2.9	2.16
3.5	2.9			
3.6	2.13			
3.7	2.13			
3.8	2.13	2.14		
3.9	2.20	3.1		
4.1	3.4	3.1	3.2	
4.2	3.3	3.5		
4.3	3.5			
4.4	3.5			
4.5	3.6			
4.6	3.9			
4.7	3.14			
4.8	3.14			
4.9	3.17			
5.1	2.15			
5.2	3.19			
5.3	3.19			
5.4	3.19			
5.5	3.18			
5.6	4.19			
5.7	4.19			
6.1	3.22			
6.2	3.22			
6.3	3.23			
6.4	3.30	4.6		
6.5	4.7			
6.6	4.8			
6.7	4.10			
6.8	4.11			

.

Part and Chapter in this book	Part and Chapter in *A History of the English Church and People*	
7.1	3.23	
7.2	4.23	
7.3	3.25	
7.4	3.25	
7.5	3.25	
7.6	3.25	
7.7	3.25	
7.8	3.25	3.26
7.9	3.26	4.4
7.10	4.23	
7.11	4.24	
7.12	4.24	
8.1	4.1	
8.2	4.1	4.2
8.3	4.2	
8.4	4.5	
8.5	4.5	
8.6	4.5	
8.7	4.17	
8.8	4.21	5.8
9.1	3.21	
9.2	3.24	
9.3	3.24	4.3
9.4	4.2	4.3
9.5	4.3	
9.6	4.3	
9.7	6.3	4.12
9.8	5.13	
9.9	5.1	
9.10	5.19	
10.1	5.19	
10.2	5.19	
10.3	5.19	
10.4	4.12	5.19

Bede: Celtic and Roman Christianity in Britain

Part and Chapter in this book	Part and Chapter in *A History of the English Church and People*
10.5	4.13 5.19
10.6	5.19
12.1	5.2
12.2	5.3
12.3	5.4
12.4	5.5
12.5	5.6
12.6	5.6
13.1	4.3 5.9 5.19
13.2	5.9 5.10
13.3	5.9
13.4	5.10

.

Part and Chapter in this book	Chapter in *Life of Cuthbert*
11.1	1
11.2	4
11.3	6
11.4	8
11.5	9
11.6	10
11.7	16
11.8	17, 18
11.9	19
11.10	20
11.11	18, 22
11.12	22
11.13	22, 24
11.14	24, 26
11.15	28
11.16	34, 36, 37
11.17	37
11.18	37
11.19	37
11.20	39
11.21	39
11.22	39, 40

Part and Chapter in this book	Part and Chapter in *Lives of the Abbots of Wearmouth and Jarrow*
14.1	1
14.2	2
14.3	2, 3
14.4	3, 4
14.5	5
14.6	6
14.7	7
14.8	8
14.9	9, 12
14.10	10
14.11	11
14.12	11
14.13	12, 13, 14
15.1	15
15.2	15
15.3	15
15.4	16
15.5	17
15.6	10, 21, 22
15.7	18